## PRAISE FOR *REDEEMING RELATIONSHIPS*

Rarely do you find a self-help book that feels like an old friend. Marty and Rich have combined warm Chicken Soup-type stories with honest personal anecdotes to create a kind of encyclopedia of help for real conflicts you and I face in our homes, at work, and in our communities. This isn't a one-size fits all solution for conflict. It's a wise and caring approach to how everyday people can redeem what conflict has ruined.

—Reno Hoff, Ph. D.
President, Corban College

I just finished Marty and Rich's book, and I will use this tool in my counseling practice today! This book is sound, funny, informative and easy to read. It is rare to find a book that encompasses and embraces the mind and heart of God while fleshing out biblical texts with proven steps used in the ministries of two transparent men (and their families). I admire both Rich and Marty for how graciously they help people redeem relationships—a graciousness of which I have been a recipient.

—K. Ellen Jacobs, MA
Family Counselor
Salem Heights Church

*Redeeming Relationships* provides practical wisdom in helping us protect and nurture our interpersonal relationships. Praise the Lord for the encouragement and support from Rich and Marty to many of us over the years.

—Sheldon C. Nord, Ph.D.
Vice President for Student Affairs
Eastern Oregon University

Drs. Rollins and Trammell have combined 50+ years of counseling with a no-nonsense and faith-filled approach to create an enjoyable read filled with practical, down-to-earth thoughts on how to redeem the relationships which fill—and fulfill—our lives. Whether in marital or managerial settings, applying the ideas behind *Redeeming Relationships* will ensure that each of us fuels the growth necessary for our relationships to thrive.

—Chuck Lucas, Christian Lawyer
Salem, Oregon

As a woman who has worked in college residence life, academics and administration, I have benefited immensely from reading *Redeeming Relationships*. I only wish it had been written many years ago. It is a practical handbook filled with relevant illustrations, biblical principles and guidelines for developing, maintaining and enriching relationships in all walks of life. I cannot think of anyone who would not benefit from reading this carefully written book. Read it and be challenged, encouraged and ready to experience the warmth of more meaningful friendships.

—Nancy Martyn
Vice President of Adult Studies
Corban College

READER BEWARE: If you want to stay mired in relational conflicts, DON'T READ THIS BOOK! As another one who, along with these authors, has "made every mistake in the book," I found *Redeeming Relationships* a careful and compassionate melding of the rock solid wisdom of God's Word with everyday experiences of two men I've seen in action for two decades. They practice what they preach, and they present real life (not simply a set of abstractions).

Rich and Marty's differences bring a richness and color to resolving relational conflict. This book will be a great keep-on-your-desk-kind of reference book for anyone willing to listen.

—Tim L. Anderson, Ph.D.
Chairman, Evangelical Theological Society

We'll spend hours fixing a broken chair, but then not take the time to heal a broken relationship. As you read this book you'll realize the immense and eternal value of your relationships. More than that, you'll learn how to restore and enrich these valuable treasures. Time invested in applying the truth of this book will bring exponential yields.

—Greg Trull, Ph.D.
Chair, Ministries Department, Corban College
Senior Pastor, Valley Baptist Church

Familiar, yet fresh … and simple, yet profound are words that came to mind as I interacted with *Redeeming Relationships*. Rich and Marty offer practical and biblical suggestions to strengthen virtually any relationship.

—Bill Katip, Ph.D.
Robert Morris University

Rich Rollins and Marty Trammell have blended fifty years of counseling experience to develop a practical and easy-to-read approach to one of the greatest challenges we face: how to create and maintain meaningful relationships with those around us. Anyone with friends, family, or co-workers should read this book.

—Chuck Lind
General Counsel and Executive Director
of Labor Relations, Kent School District

# REDEEMING
# RELATIONSHIPS

To Mark

Thank you so much
for your help

Rich

How to Resolve

10 Common Conflicts

(and reduce their frequency!)

# REDEEMING
# RELATIONSHIPS

Marty Trammell, Ph.D.
Rich Rollins, D.Min

FaithWalk
PUBLISHING
Grand Haven, Michigan

Published by FaithWalk Publishing
Grand Haven, Michigan 49417

Printed in the United States of America
12 11 10 09 08 07          7 6 5 4 3 2 1

Library of Congress Cataloging-in-Publication Data

Rollins, Rich.
  Redeeming relationships : how to resolve 10 common conflicts (and reduce their frequency!) / by Rich Rollins & Marty Trammell.
     p. cm.
  Includes bibliographical references (p 206).
  ISBN-13: 978-1-932902-66-2 (pbk. : alk. paper)
  ISBN-10: 1-932902-66-X
  1. Interpersonal conflict—Religious aspects—Christianity. I. Trammell, Marty.
II. Title.
  BV4597.53.C58R65 2007
  158.2—dc22
                        2006038350

# DEDICATION

To LouAnna Rollins and Linda Trammell,
and to our children,
Rebecca, Jennifer, Andrew, Justin, Chris, and Josh.

Your love, laughter, forgiveness, and faith have continued
to remind us that relationships are worth redeeming.

This book is for anyone who has ever hoped to make a
relationship work—for anyone who has ever longed to
trade conflict for closeness.

# CONTENTS

# FOREWORD

A warm summer breeze carries the laughter of a little brother pushed in a swing by his big sister. "Higher! Higher! Whooooo!" Neither of them would rather be anywhere else in the world.

A glance from a photo frame reminds a husband of his true love. He drifts from desk to home. His work brings his body to the office, but his heart never leaves home.

A yearning groan rises from a prayerful huddle. Young and old, black and white, Pierre Cardin and pierced noses all bent at the knee and in the heart. The reality of something, Someone, greater fades the differences and sharpens the focus. You are more important than me and He is more important than both of us.

The Hebrew Scripture writers called it shalom. Simply translated "peace," it's when everything is as it should be. Deep in our souls we all long for it. Too often it eludes.

In my years as a senior pastor and college professor I've found that one obstacle more than any other keeps people from finding true peace: the inability to resolve conflict. Imagine if you, your children, your church, your co-workers could face the inevitable clashes of life and from them grow in the faith. That conflict's heat could be harnessed to temper and strengthen rather than consume and weaken. That after the smoke clears, people love deeper. Impossible? Maybe, maybe not.

This book stems from two husbands and leaders who have learned about harnessing conflict to the glory of God and the building of relationships. If you weary of untested theories or ivory tower pronouncements, read this book. Its words will transform you, because they flow from changed

XIII

lives. I have known the authors and their families for many years—they're for real. They've struggled where we all struggle and now share with us what really works.

Greg Trull, Ph.D.
Chair, Ministries Department, Corban College
Senior Pastor, Valley Baptist Church, Perrydale, Oregon

# Acknowledgments

**Special thanks (from Rich) to**

My parents, sister, and brother-in-law:

Harold (who is with the Lord) and Berniece, in whom I always saw Christ and without whose constant encouragement and prayer I would have never been in full-time ministry. Barbara and Jerry for their constant belief in me.

My colleagues during my time at Corban College:

Dr. Tom Younger (who is with the Lord), Dr. John Balyo, Dr. Bill Katip, Dr. Sheldon Nord, Keith Cox, Nancy Martyn, and Anne Jeffers, whose relational commitment gave me insight and encouragement to begin to write my thoughts.

My colleagues at Valley Bible Church:

Pastors Dr. Phillip Howard, Ted Montoya, David Hurtado, David Howard, along with Donna Tanguay, Angela Vedar, Ron Hughes, and the rest of our wonderful staff, who have encouraged me to keep writing and teaching.

My special encouragers:

Jack Werre, Keith Cox, Pastor Keith Crome, and Chuck Lind, whom God used many times to encourage a discouraged pastor and friend.

The Valley Bible Congregation:

Who have sacrificially loved and supported a pastor in the trenches of urban life.

My reader/researcher:

Kevin Straugh, whose insight and hard work made this book a better one.

**Special thanks (from Marty) to**

My friend and literary agent:

David Sanford, whose friendship encouraged my past thirty-five years and convinced me to begin a writing ministry.

My pastors:

James Godwin, Donn Mogford, David Miller, Tom Younger, and Greg Trull, whose relentless commitment to relationships inspired many of these pages.

My family:

The Trammells and Markwoods, whose prayers pushed the keys when I was too tired to type.

My colleagues, students, and friends at Corban College and Valley Baptist of Perrydale:

Dr. Linda Samek, Dr. Bryce Bernard, Dr. Greg Trull, Dr. Roy Bunch, Dr. Rich Meyers, Dr. Colette Tennant, Christena Brooks, Anne Jeffers, Nancy Martyn, Paul Meyers, Bob and Rose Gillette, Ellen Jacobs, and my writing mentor, Jim Hills, whose counsel redeemed these pages.

**Special thanks (from both of us) to**

Our editors from Sanford Communications:

Elizabeth Jones, whose timely, wise and cheerful advice kept our dream alive, and to David Sanford, Rebekah Clark, and Elizabeth Honeycutt for their assistance.

Our colleagues at FaithWalk Publishing:

Publisher Dirk Wierenga, editor Louann Werksma, and production manager Ginny McFadden, whose belief in these pages and professional expertise gave substance to this dream.

Most of all, we thank the Redeemer of Relationships himself. May we know the closeness he desires for us all.

Warmly,

Rich and Marty

# Introduction:
# In the Shallow End

*Authors' Note: Many stories in this book are composites of real-life experiences and are thus fictional. In those cases that are actual, we have changed the person's name. When we share our own experiences, our names appear at the beginning in parentheses.*

When I (Marty) was six years old, my mom took me to swim lessons. The water in the shallow end threatened every breath as it lapped just beneath my chin. As long as I could touch both of my feet to the prickly, concrete bottom and hang close to the side of the pool, I felt safe.

As I stood there with my hair dry and my hands just a few feet from the pool's edge, another breed of kid played at the other end. I watched with jealous wonder as these kids splashed around and jumped off the diving board one after the other, like penguins on a grand adventure. Some of them even dove beneath the surface of the water and swam gracefully in what seemed like a whole new world to me. I wanted so much to swim out there too, but I knew the water was over my head, so I stayed where I was safe.

After each swim lesson, I promised myself that I'd venture out to the deep the very next week. But the lesson would come and, before I could muster up enough courage to inch my way out, the instructor would blow her whistle and I'd be left standing with my hair dry as a growing crowd of kids pushed past me, up the stairs, and out of the pool.

Not much has changed. Oh, I'm not afraid of pools anymore. Now I'm afraid of people. Maybe we all are. After all, there is something unsettling about entering the deep places of the human spirit. Sure, we want to enjoy the deep waters of real and engaging friendship, but we're afraid of getting in over our heads. It seems so much safer to keep our feet down against the bottom of the pool.

Jesus Christ never said that following him was about staying safe. He never wanted us to settle for watching the swimmers at the other end. He showed us that relationships are about getting our hair wet and jumping off the board and diving deep into *another* world.

Yes, there are wonders in *this* world. There are mountains and manatees and media and museums that fill our days with delight. But let us never forget that although these are meant for our pleasure, we are meant for relationship. That's all that carries over into God's other world—the wonder of one another—the wonder that can only be explored if we leave the safety of the shallow end.

## RELATIONAL CONFLICT

We have found through our fifty-plus years of combined pastoral counseling experience that relational conflict is a primary reason people stay in the shallows. In the Gospel of John, Jesus prayed that Christians would experience such unity that the world would notice and be drawn toward him. He prayed that his followers "may be one ... so that the world may believe that you have sent me" (17:21).

Most of us want these kinds of relationships, but the conflicts are too much with us. The days that used to make us smile are gone and the only *Happy Days* in our lives are in the reruns we rent from Netflix™. We feel consumed by relational conflicts that confine our hearts and minds to the shallow end. Like the people in the following three scenarios, we're looking for solutions.

## Sounds Familiar

*"When I repress my emotions, my stomach keeps score."*
—John Powell

Sitting in her Lexus after fleeing the attorney's office, Amy wondered how she got to this place. If someone had told her eight years before that her marriage would end in divorce, she would never have believed it. She reflected back—way back.

Alex and Amy had been childhood sweethearts. They appeared to have an ideal relationship. Alex was a Tom Cruise lookalike with a successful career as a stockbroker. Amy had been a homecoming princess and a salutatorian.

Soon after their well attended wedding, Amy began working in real estate, mostly because Alex did not want "three kids and a Dalmatian" right away. Amy obtained her broker's license and launched out on her own. Where most realtors concentrated on home sales, Amy tackled the commercial market. Soon she found that selling commercial property was not only exciting, but also lucrative.

Their first major disagreement came over having children. Amy wanted to begin a family as soon as they married. Alex argued that they needed time to become acquainted as husband and wife. Amy saw the logic in Alex's position. But, after several years, it became apparent that Alex had never intended to become a father.

As the logic behind becoming "better acquainted" dissipated, so did their happiness. Several years into their marriage, they stopped discussing the matter and began to retreat into separate worlds.

Still, Alex and Amy seemed happy. They were successful. They were the envy of their circle of friends. Yet they were lonely. Like the "nowhere man" in the classic rock song, Alex and Amy felt like they "were making all [their] nowhere plans for nobody."

One gray, rain-soaked morning, after a week of little interaction with Alex, Amy decided to retain an attorney. Alex found out and, without telling her, met her at the attorney's office. Amy was caught off guard and flew into a rage. An embarrassing exchange took place in the waiting room, and Amy fled the building with Alex close behind. He broke off the chase when Amy climbed into her Lexus and started the engine.

She sat stunned, wondering, "How?"

"What went wrong?"

What went wrong? It's a good question. It's the same question that Sheila asked after being fired from what she thought was a secure job. She assumed that because she was a gifted computer programmer, she had a job for life. However, Sheila underestimated the importance of getting along with others. She didn't realize that most people lose their jobs not because of technical incompetence, but because they create relational conflict.

Over the years, Sheila had developed the bad habit of having to be right in every argument. When she won an argument, she felt better about herself. What she didn't realize was that she was the only one who felt "better." Eventually, her colleagues left her alone. She began to feel like a celibate priest at a couple's retreat. Sheila worked every day without the sense of humor and the give-and-take flexibility so necessary to the life of a team. Left out socially and professionally, it was only a matter of time before she would lose her enthusiasm—and her job.

Her last evaluation should have been a warning. It ended by stating, "Sheila is a skilled programmer but has a difficult time fitting into the project development team." She remembered it as she sat in the parking structure wondering how she would tell her husband Tim that she had lost her job. Little did she realize that Tim would understand—he had never won an argument, either.

Several miles away, in a 12-year-old Taurus, sat Fred Cranston. Pastor Cranston had been at New Haven Community Church for four years. He was a gifted speaker and teacher. In the forty-two years the church existed, it had never had a pastor who knew the Bible as well as Fred. Graduating at the top of his seminary class, Fred was in demand. However, three pastorates later, he found himself in the church parking lot, wondering what had happened.

He had just left a short meeting with Neal, the chairman of his board. Neal's words hurt: "Pastor, people feel that they have no say in matters. They are afraid to disagree with you. The board feels, after discussing it with the church, that if you stay we will continue to lose families. Soon we will be unable to pay your salary."

Fred remembered the event that led to the board meeting. In a discussion about a new building program, conflict arose over the configuration of the parking lot. Despite Fred's seminary training in alleviating conflict, no one agreed with his point of view. Since he had been taught that the pastor was "always right," Fred accused the church members of "sinning." The accusation led to his being asked to resign.

## IT'S EVERYWHERE

Fred's, Sheila's, and Alex and Amy's experiences are not unusual. Ask any police officer about domestic conflict and he or she will tell you that unresolved conflict is tearing apart the fabric of many homes. According to statistics, over half of America's married couples in the 1990s found themselves filing for divorce. Ask human resources professionals and they will tell you that unresolved conflict can cost us jobs and ruin our chances of succeeding in business. We all know of extremely bright people who are unable to begin new relationships or obtain employment because their reputation precedes them.

We find conflict at the kitchen table, in the corporate office, on the ball field, the golf course, the freeway, or at the health club—none of our relationships are exempt. Every parent, every child, every spouse, every employer— every one of us has experienced the crippling effects of unresolved conflict.

But conflict need not cripple us. Although it may be one of the most difficult things we do in life, resolving conflict is also one of the most rewarding. As we begin our journey through this emotional labyrinth, we will discover practical solutions, as well as ways to reduce the frequency of the conflicts we face.

Since the Bible contains God's wisdom about both the causes of conflict and how to resolve them, we have worked hard to let Scripture outline the content of this book. We are not "self-appointed experts." We are pastors who help people with their conflicts, and we are individuals learning to solve our own. It's our prayer that you will find, in these pages, the help and courage you need to let go of the side and swim deep.

## CHAPTER ONE

# SOLUTION

## DEALING WITH NEEDS AND WANTS

Experience is the best teacher—especially other people's experiences!

The good news? The two of us have already made every mistake in the book. Take our word for it: The best thing you can do is discard any misconceptions you may have about relational conflicts, arguments, and disagreements.

I (Rich) can still remember the morning when Dave, a close friend, took me to breakfast and proceeded to confront me about the way I treated people. I sat there and listened to him because I knew Dave loved me. He had earned the right to confront me. I am in ministry today, in part, due to his confrontation. I thank the Lord I have been married for several decades. Yet, without Dave's love for me and his courage to say something, I doubt my wife LouAnna and I would have made it.

Dave risked our relationship. I am a strong-willed individual. Ask my friends; they will tell you that when operating outside of the Spirit's control, I have an opinion on everything. I will reduce everything to an opportunity to win. My attitude forced everyone around me to "walk on eggshells." One of my coworkers said that having a relationship with me was like "kissing a sparkplug."

Yet Dave loved me enough to wade in and confront me. I left that confrontation so angry I had to collect myself before I could drive out of the restaurant parking lot. I vowed to never speak to him again. Yet, over the next several days, God used the event to bring me to my knees. I couldn't get past Dave's words because I knew how much he loved me and how hard that conversation was for him.

## EXPLODE THE MYTHS OF RELATIONAL CONFLICT

Most of us have probably felt this sting from what Scripture calls the "faithful wound of a friend" (Proverbs 27:6). But as we have discovered in our years of counseling, most of us find it easier to lick our wounds rather than learn from them. Redeeming relationships requires us to stop licking and start learning. Exploding the myths about relational conflict is the best place to begin.

### Myth #1: My relationships will succeed without confrontation

One of the hidden scars of unresolved conflict is disunity. It's true that, for a short time, avoiding conflict can make us feel like we're flying down the superhighway of life, the wind in our hair and our low-profile Michelins barely touching the pavement. Then a huge pothole appears ("out of nowhere" we swear). Suddenly we're faced with the insurmountable truth—there can be no lasting success in a relationship based on pretense: No matter how much we want to believe the myth, conflict will not take care of itself. That's where the rubber really meets the road.

Jesus knew this. Buried in the passionate prose of John 17, where Jesus Christ prayed that Christians would be "one," lays a deep concern: He asks his father, God, to "protect us from the evil one" (Satan). This protection promotes the kind of affectionate unity that draws people toward God (John 17:20–23). What is one of the tactics of the evil one? He convinces us that we can succeed without facing and fixing relational conflict.

Earlier, Jesus had given careful instructions about this: "Therefore, if you are offering your gift at the altar and there remember that your brother has something against you, leave your gift there in front of the altar. First go and be reconciled to your brother; then come and offer your gift" (Matthew 5:23–24). He knew we'd be able to convince ourselves that we can succeed without redeeming our relationships. But, as General Douglas MacArthur so aptly put it in the midst of his greatest relational conflict, "nothing could be further from the truth."

## Myth #2: Disagreement is sin

I (Rich) had been the dean of students in a Christian liberal arts college in the Northwest for several years when I encountered Eric. In a casual conversation in my office, Eric, a freshman, expressed some strong disagreements about some of the college's policies. My response surprised him.

"I don't like some of them either. Let's compare notes and see if our lists are the same."

I knew Eric's family background. He came from a home where to ask "why?" was tantamount to rebellion. I always sensed that Eric wanted to be obedient, but he also wanted to know the basis of the rules in his house. Like many of us in our overly analytical teen years, he saw a disparity between what was taught in the Bible and what was practiced in the home.

Since his father would explode at him during their disagreements, Eric learned to disagree in the same fashion. Neither Eric nor his father had a clue that the sin in disagreement is often in *how* we disagree. When we shout, change the subject, dredge up the past, stomp off, manipulate with tears, hit, retreat to silence, blame, use sarcasm, humiliate, or threaten to leave the person, we are sinning. Learning how to disagree is far more important than trying to avoid all disagreement. Allowing people to disagree with us gives them the freedom to bring the conflict out into the open. It allows the participants to seek resolution and growth.

God's Word models this for us. The Bible contains an entire genre of Psalms called "Lament Psalms." These Psalms include sentences such as "Why, O Lord, do you stand far off? Why do you hide yourself in times of trouble?" (10:1) and "Hear me, O God, as I voice my complaint" (64:1). Was it wrong or sinful for the Psalm writers to express their personal conflicts with God? It sure doesn't look like it!

What God seems to be reminding us is the fact that such feelings are real and need to be communicated. Notice how these same Psalms resolve: "You hear, O Lord, the desire of the afflicted; you encourage them, and you listen to their cry" (10:17); and "Let the righteous rejoice in the Lord and take refuge in him" (64:10). C. S. Lewis said that, in these psalms, a person sees in print a feeling we all know too well: "Resentment, expressing itself with perfect freedom, without disguise, without self-consciousness, without shame—as few but children would express it today."[1] The point? If a personal conflict with God is not sin, then conflicts with his creatures aren't sinful, either. It is what we do with the conflict that makes the difference!

Perhaps one of the greatest lessons that parents, children, friends, pastors, teachers, and employers must learn is this: Allowing individuals to express their feelings about conflict (in an appropriate manner) can help them move toward resolution. Personal conflicts shouldn't be labeled "sin."

### Myth #3: I can still grow without resolving conflict

It turned out that young Eric was angry about one specific area of standards at the college. The college required all freshmen students to live in the college residence halls. In addition, each student who didn't choose a specific roommate was assigned one. If a roommate conflict arose (and they often did), we would not consider changing roommates until the two had gone through a series of controlled confrontations and exercises together.

"I'm old enough to vote—I shouldn't have to be told where to live," Eric retorted. "Besides, my roommate is a jerk."

"What does he think of you?" I asked.

"I don't know ... he probably thinks I'm the jerk."

I put my hand on his shoulder. "I know this is a tough experience, but will you sit down and talk? I don't know if I can satisfy your concerns, but I can help you understand how this standard can benefit you in your education."

During the next hour I shared with him the results of national studies that demonstrated that in nearly every area—emotionally, socially, academically, and spiritually— the on-campus freshman excels over the off-campus freshman.

Eric was a typical private college student. He had never shared a room. Sharing space for the first time was one of the most difficult things he had done. He finally confessed that most of the time he liked his roommate, but that the night before they had "blown-up" at each other.

"Are you willing to talk to him about these things?" I asked.

"I think that if I really told him what I feel, he'd be hurt." His shoulders relaxed and a previously hidden compassion crept into his words.

I've heard this excuse many times when dealing with fractured relationships, but withholding the truth can also mean refusing to love. John Powell affirms this notion:

> Most of us feel that others will not tolerate such emotional honesty in communication. We would rather defend our

dishonesty on the grounds that it might hurt others; and, having rationalized our phoniness into nobility, we settle for superficial relationships.[2]

Had Eric taken this immaturity with his roommate into his marriage, he would have left for the reason many couples do—unresolved conflict. It's difficult to experience the blessings that personal growth brings to our relationships if we don't resolve our conflicts.

## Myth #4: Real love doesn't confront; it forgives

The greatest love we show doesn't end at forgiveness. It ends at the truth. We want it to be delivered with kindness, gentleness, and concern, but we want it said. When we refuse to confront because we think we should be more forgiving, we are saying that we do not really love the other person.

Our culture doesn't help much. We have been brought up with the idea that true love only forgives. Like the characters in Henrik Ibsen's play, *The Wild Duck*, we are consumed with the idea that telling the truth will always lead to more pain. We feel we are cursed ("thirteenth at the table") if we dare try to help someone walk into and through a time of conflict. But, unlike the ending of Ibsen's play, Scripture reminds us that conflict doesn't have to consume and condemn.

The Apostle Paul explained to the first-century church in Galatia that, along with forgiving people, we are to help those who are struggling—even if it initially creates more conflict (Galatians 6:1). We are to confront them in love, just as we would hope to be confronted. This is the context for the next, and much loved, verse: "Carry each other's burdens, and in this way you will fulfill the law of Christ" (6:2). Initially confrontation creates some conflict, but when the confrontation contains commitment, it also creates a new sense and degree of caring.

I (Marty) often face this uncomfortable task in my office at the college. One day I'm confronting the manipulation that seems to haunt "late" assignments, the next it's a lack of friendliness between roommates. Although the confrontations rarely start well, they rarely end poorly. Those awkward times not only help the students, they also bring a new dimension to my relationships—to my ideas about "caring" and the "law of Christ." It's one thing to forgive and quite another to share the world of caring that lies just beyond forgiveness.

Both of us have worked with hundreds of Erics over the years. Most of these roommates have, by the end of the year, become inseparable. In fact, in Eric's case, a decade later he and his roommate are still best friends. Real love doesn't just forgive; it confronts.

## Myth #5: Agreement is the glue of unity

This myth is often translated, "If I disagree with her, she will leave me." LouAnna and I (Rich) have been married for more than forty years now. We are a great team. We are united over the main issues. There are still many things, however, about which we disagree. We decided long ago that we are not going to let our disagreements divide us. We resolve those that are important. We "live and let live" those that are not important.

In my present ministry, I have had the pleasure of working with an individual who played for the NFL. When discussing this fact, he commented that every football team is made up of players who have their own ideas about how the team should function. Their differences add strength to the team. The quarterback sees the game from his perspective. The lineman sees the game from his perspective. They don't always agree on what's important or what the next play should be. But when the play is called, they each do their part to make the team a success.

Unity is not dependent upon agreement.

## Myth #6: It is easier to put up with a conflict than to resolve it

Good decisions are not measured on the basis of the ease with which they are made, but on the effectiveness of their outcome. Yet many of our decisions are based on whether they are convenient. We tend to avoid decisions that may make waves.

One of my (Rich's) friends has a daughter we will call Brenda. She is in her late thirties. She remains at home with her parents, not because she is unemployable and not because of the cost of living on her own. Brenda lives with them because she does not want to work. She went off to college, graduated, came home, and has been there ever since.

Not only does Brenda not work, she does not participate in the duties and responsibilities around the home. When dinner is ready, she shows up, she eats, and then retreats back to her sitcoms while her mom clears the table and washes the dishes. Both of her parents are intelligent people. Both are angry with her, but she doesn't know it.

When I asked what they were going to do about it, their response indicated that they were afraid to do anything. This was their daughter and they felt responsible for her well-being. If they "made waves" she would react and make their lives miserable. If they kicked her out, which is what they wanted to do, she would merely become a "street person." Many of us view our relationships the same way. We feel it is easier to put up with conflict than resolve it.

In 1994, my wife noticed that a small dot on my back seemed to be growing larger and darker. For several months I simply dismissed it as one of hundreds of freckles dotting my body. It was easier to put up with it than to make the effort to change my schedule and get an appointment to see my doctor. On Thanksgiving of that year she measured it and took a picture. Within a few weeks, it had grown noticeably larger. A week before Christmas I had it removed. On January 3, I received a call from the physician instructing me to come into his office. When I suggested that the first opening I had in my schedule was several weeks from then, he said, "I'll see you in my office tomorrow morning at 8:30!"

The next day LouAnna and I sat in the dermatologist's office as he told me that he had removed a metastatic melanoma. He said he "hoped" that he had gotten all of it. I learned that if it spread to other organs, there was almost no hope for recovery. Something I was willing to "put up with" almost killed me. I did not like the message he gave, but as a physician he was willing to tell me the truth rather than tell me what I wanted to hear. In the same way, Brenda needs parents who are willing to resolve the conflict, rather than put up with it.

## Myth #7: Treating the symptoms can solve the conflict

I (Rich) have struggled with being overweight most of my adult life. I have tried every diet known to humanity. Some years ago I realized that my obesity was a symptom of my lifestyle. Like any symptom, unless you treat the cause, you have little hope of ever winning the battle. I had always tried to lose weight without changing the way I lived. So when I did lose weight, I immediately went back to eating and living like I have always eaten and lived. As a result, I gained much of my weight back.

Several years ago I began slowly changing my lifestyle to incorporate more exercise. I began cutting out unhealthy foods. I discovered that the portions I ate were too large and so I began to eat smaller portions. I quit weighing myself every day. My goal became healthy living rather than losing weight. The side benefit was that I lost weight!

If we view conflict the same way, we discover some significant insights. Conflict—like my weight—is merely a symptom of a deeper cause. I can chase after conflicts with every new diet, temporarily losing pounds and inches, or I can address the cause and change the reason I eat. Treating the symptom isn't the same as solving the conflict.

## Myth #8: I can ignore what's important to me

Our willingness to be in conflict is directly proportional to how strongly we feel about a particular need or want. Famed psychologist Abraham Maslow diagrammed our needs and wants this way:

Simply stated, Maslow believed that perceived needs can be categorized into groups. These groups are hierarchical in nature. Until our physiological needs (food, clothing and shelter) are met, we cannot focus on the next level of need (safety). The need for safety, in turn, must be met before we are able to move to the next step and meet our need to belong and be loved, and so forth.

Why is this important? It is important because so often we convince ourselves that we can ignore the feelings we attach to our needs and wants. The eighteen-year-old who fears being asked to provide for himself or herself for the first time is less concerned about being loved and belonging. He or she is concerned with the basics. The parents may miss this point and wonder why their love and the warmth of family are rebuffed by the teen.

## NEEDS AND WANTS

We have found through the years that ignoring or mis-understanding needs and wants is the cause of considerable conflict in families, corporations, and community organizations. No matter how hard we try not to, we eventually react when we don't get what we need or want. We can try to bench our frustration, but it won't stay seated. The resulting irritableness shakes up our lives and pressurizes our emotions like carbonation in a soda pop can, ready to explode at the next person who pulls our lid. It may sound like a Yogi Berra-ism, but the truth is, we can't ignore what we can't ignore. Here's another example followed by a simple exercise we can use to help us recognize which needs and wants are contributing to the relational conflicts in our lives.

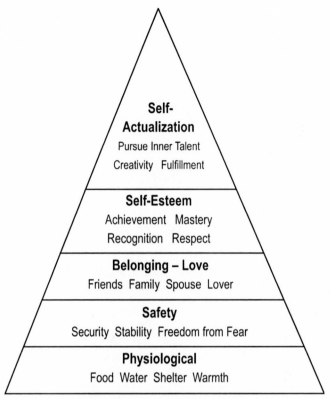

**Self-Actualization**
Pursue Inner Talent
Creativity  Fulfillment

**Self-Esteem**
Achievement  Mastery
Recognition  Respect

**Belonging – Love**
Friends  Family  Spouse  Lover

**Safety**
Security  Stability  Freedom from Fear

**Physiological**
Food  Water  Shelter  Warmth

**Maslow's Hierarchy of Human Needs**

While working in health care, one of our medical directors came into my (Rich's) office and slumped down in a chair. "I need a Ferrari," he said. I shifted a stack of medical journals, "Nobody needs a Ferrari. What you need is transportation, but what you want is a Ferrari."

My response made sense to me. So much sense that I shared my wisdom with my wife that evening. Her only comment, while folding another faded bath towel, was, "Then why do we have a Porsche?"

Why is it always easier to recognize the conflicts caused by other people's needs and wants than it is to recognize our own? One of the best exercises a person can do is to begin three lists. (See chart on the next page.) This exercise can help us recognize the needs and wants in our lives that create conflicts with others. Recognizing the role these needs and wants play can help us redeem relationships, as well as reduce the frequency of conflicts we experience.

---

### Changing the Frequency: Needs, Wants, and Relationships

1. Create three columns on a piece of paper.

2. List your needs in the left column.

3. List your wants in the right column.

4. List the relationship-oriented conflicts you are facing in the middle.

5. Look for relationships between the three lists you've compiled (especially lists 3 and 4).

Seeing the relationships between needs, wants, and conflicts can help you become more sensitive to the root cause. This can help you understand why you are facing conflict in a relationship.

---

Anyone who completes this simple activity will find that often our conflicts are caused by unmet needs, frustrated feelings about things we want, or misunderstandings (ours and others) about what our real needs are.

As we learn to understand the effects produced by our feelings about our needs and wants, we'll become more aware of how needs and wants affect the emotional states of the people around us. Understanding these impacts will help us resolve interpersonal conflicts, but first we have to explode the myths: Conflict resolution isn't an option if we continue to think we can ignore what we can't ignore. Learning the impact of needs and wants can help us redeem our relationships.

BOLD IDEAS

Most of us find it easier to lick our wounds rather than learn from them.

Withholding the truth can also mean refusing to love.

Learning how to disagree is far more important than trying to avoid all disagreement.

We feel it is easier to put up with conflict than resolve it.

We can't ignore what we can't ignore.

Unity is not dependent upon agreement.

It's one thing to forgive and quite another to share the world of caring that lies just beyond forgiveness.

Treating the symptom isn't the same as solving the conflict.

## CHAPTER TWO

# SOLUTION

# SHRUGGERS

It's easy to confuse conflict with unpleasant circumstances. Discovering ten minutes before work that your car has a flat tire or finding a Lego® in your USB port are frustrating events, but they're not the types of conflicts we are writing about. These trials do wear on us, like waves on the seashore, but we have little—if any—control over them.

Relational conflicts, however, are not waves. They are tsunamis that lash at the foundation of our friendships and our faith. This kind of conflict can wash us away—unless we learn how to weather the storms.

## SHRUGGERS

When a thunderstorm is brewing outside, the best response is to come inside, out of the rain. Some of the tumultuous conflicts we encounter are not ours to solve. God doesn't expect us to do anything about them—except avoid them! They are what we call "shruggers."

The shrugger is what King Solomon had in mind when he wrote in the biblical book of Proverbs: "Like one who seizes a dog by the ears is a passer-by who meddles in a quarrel not his own" (Proverbs 26:17).

Meddling in a quarrel when we should shrug and walk away can have dangerous results, but it's the kind of thing we often do. Some of us seem to *attract* conflict. Like tube socks in the static-cling of life, every testy situation around us ends up sticking to us. We grimace, knowing we are about to grab another dog by the ears, but even anticipating the pain isn't enough to make us let go. Instead of evaluating the situation and shrugging, we embrace it. And after all is said and done we wonder, "What went wrong?"

Whatever you do today, remember this: solving conflict involves learning to shrug. The Apostle Paul gives us some practical counsel on such matters:

> Carry each other's burdens, and in this way you will fulfill the law of Christ. If anyone thinks he is something when he is nothing, he deceives himself. Each one should test his own actions. Then he can take pride in himself, without comparing himself to somebody else, for each one should carry his own load (Galatians 6:2–5).

The word "burdens" commonly refers to something that is too heavy to carry alone. It must be carried by two or more people. The word "load" in verse 5 refers to something carried by one person. When we encounter people with life's burdens, Paul is implying that we must wisely determine which burden or load they have. Is this a burden too great for them to carry alone or is this a load that they must alone bear? When it is the latter, our response should not be to carry the load for them, but to come alongside and help them discover the skills and wisdom they need to carry the "load" themselves. This concept is especially difficult for two types of people—problem-solvers and rescuers.

## PROBLEM-SOLVERS

If you find it difficult to listen to a problem without diving in with a sure fix, you're a problem-solver and may not have learned how to shrug yet. The solution is to realize that some problems have a divine purpose—and that purpose might be to help the person who has the problem.

In Jane Austen's classic novel *Pride and Prejudice,* the unscrupulous and manipulative Mr. Wickham convinces Lizzy that his misfortune is the result of Mr. Darcy's cruelty and selfishness. Although the accusation isn't true, Lizzy shares it with her family. Blinded by the allegation, Lizzy and the Bennett family allow Lydia to be swept off her feet by Mr. Wickham. Driven by lust and greed, he runs away with Lydia, creating a scandalous situation for the Bennetts. Mr. Darcy, despite being maligned by the Bennetts, comes to their rescue by paying Mr. Wickham to marry Lydia, thereby saving the family's reputation. Although Austen leaves out the rest of the story about Mr. Wickham and Lydia (probably because the result of a match made in money is not much of a prospect for a "romantic" ending), she does leave the reader with a feeling of foreboding about their hapless future. The novel continues, instead, with the romance of Lizzy and Mr. Darcy, a man whose character sells the story.

The point is that the situation could have been averted if Lizzy had realized Mr. Wickham's misfortune was not her problem to fix. If Lizzy would have shrugged off his manipulative attitude and words, the family would have discovered much sooner (but, of course, less tragically) the goodness in Mr. Darcy. And, even more, they would have discovered Mr. Wickham's lack of character and saved their daughter from a meaningless marriage. From this perspective, Austen's novel reminds us that failing to *shrug* can create new problems and delay the maturity that comes from learning to fix our own mistakes.

Fifty combined years of working with people have taught us that when we fail to shrug, we often make a mess of situations that were never ours to mess with in the first place. We've also learned that people need to struggle sometimes to solve their own problems. If we learn to shrug and let them struggle, they can mature. If we fail to shrug, we can hold them back from becoming the best people they can be. With a little listening and some encouragement, people will often take the right steps on their own. That's another reason it's important that we learn to shrug.

## RESCUERS

Many people spend every waking moment looking for a need to fill, not realizing that doing nothing may be the best avenue of growth and productivity.

Anna was this kind of person. Her son Tim had been imprisoned for being drunk and disorderly. Twice her close friends had advised her to leave him there without bail in the hope that the time in jail would serve to "wake him up." However, she could not bear the thought of his suffering and twice bailed him out. Tim, in fact, knew that his mom would come and continues to live a troubled life without any accountability for his actions.

In their bestselling book *Boundaries,* Drs. Cloud and Townsend warn:

> Made in the image of God, we were created to take responsibility for certain tasks. Part of taking responsibility, or ownership, is knowing what is our job, and what isn't. Workers who continually take on duties that aren't theirs will eventually burn out. It takes wisdom to know what we should be doing and what we shouldn't. We can't do everything.[1]

When we learn to shrug, we help others learn to carry their own loads—and we learn the joy and freedom of carrying our own loads, as well. When we shrug, everyone wins.

### Steps to Identifying Shruggers

When faced with a conflict in a relationship, ask these three questions:

1. How will I help this person if I intervene?
2. Is there something greater that God is trying to do here—and will my intervening get in the way?
3. If I shrug this off, what will the likely result be?

If you aren't the key to resolving a relational conflict, back off. Shrug. Let go of the dog's ears. God will come through. And, if you shrug fast enough, you just might have enough of your hand left to lend it to someone who really needs you.

## Huggers

"I wonder if you would visit my daughter in the hospital?" The phone request came from a friend with whom I (Rich) had worked while in health care. Betty was concerned for her daughter and remembered that LouAnna and I now lived in the same city.

When we visited we found a young college student who was hearing-impaired and in need of bed rest. She was not strong enough to travel 600 miles south to be with her mom. Nor did she have any friends who could help. It was obvious to us that her burden was too great for her to bear alone and we invited her to stay with us until she was strong enough to resume her life. Her conflict was a "hugger," something we needed to hold on to and support her through. She had a burden too great to carry alone.

The heavy burden will break a person if someone doesn't come to her aid. It's a load designed for two or more.

## Two Important Cautions

As we consider our response to the conflicts that surround us, it is important to be reminded of two cautions.

### #1 Majoring on the minor

Sometimes, a conflict we face is a minor one. Minor issues that do belong to us are not "shruggers," but beware of reacting in a major way to a minor issue.

Several years after graduating from college, I (Rich) worked as a medical technologist in a local hospital. The afternoon/evening shift was my favorite. I arrived one afternoon to an explosion of angry words from the outpatient waiting room. In the middle of the room stood the associate hospital administrator and my boss. Nose to nose they stood, name-calling, neither willing to back down. My gaze migrated to the patients shifting uncomfortably in the bright red chairs that lined the walls of the room. I remember feeling embarrassed for these two "adults."

The conflict involved how the chairs in the waiting room should be arranged. The administrator felt it was his responsibility to determine the outpatient waiting room layout. My boss was determined not to relinquish any ground in the matter. Everyone except these two saw this as a minor issue.

Sometime later my boss asked my opinion about the "discussion."

"If you expend that kind of energy over the placement of a few chairs, what kind of response will you have when the issue is a major one?" I asked. Disturbed that I didn't take her side in the matter, she tried to make the conflict more significant.

"What right does he have to come down here and dictate the arrangement of our outpatient room?"

For me, this minor problem was a "shrugger." For her, it was a hugger—but one she should have kept in perspective.

Several months later the administration made some demands on our area that negatively affected our work. We had no lines of communication for resolving the situation since our boss was perceived by the administration as a "reactor." This time, her legitimate complaint was ignored because she had overreacted earlier to a problem she should have labeled "minor." Whenever we respond to a minor issue in a major way, we undermine our future ability to be effective in resolving conflict.

## #2 Minoring on the major

Just as it is never wise to treat a minor conflict as a major one, it isn't helpful to treat a major conflict as if it were minor.

The Bible's dramatic love poem, the Song of Songs, describes the importance of making sure we take a serious look at conflicts in our marriages before we call them "minor." In a passage where the bride is hiding from her lover because she views herself as inadequate—as plain and ordinary—the lover warns, "catch for us the foxes, the little foxes that ruin the vineyard, our vineyard that is in bloom" (2:15).

The "little foxes" are things (like a person's view of his or her own attractiveness) that, although they appear to be "little," can ruin a relationship (the "vineyard"). Most of us would think that the large foxes (problems) would be a more serious threat, because they're large enough to eat the fruit and ruin the harvest. But the "little foxes" are actually the most dangerous because they eat at the root and destroy the entire vine. What Solomon is telling us is that the lover does not want the intoxicating nature of their new relationship (the "vineyard") to be ruined by something "major" that she thinks is "little" or minor.

When my wife and I (Marty) cover this passage in premarital counseling sessions, we usually find Solomon's point confirmed. Many women identify with the young bride in this ancient love story, but fail to realize that how they feel about their own beauty affects the flavor of their marriage.

Solomon's point is that women (and men) who treat their low opinion of their attractiveness as a minor conflict often find less intimacy in their marriages. The Lover's point is important to repeat: Make sure you catch the "little foxes," because the damage they do is major.

Rob discovered this the hard way. "Pastor, Lynn just left me ... she says she wants a divorce ... she says she can't live this way anymore." Rob was devastated. He had arrived home from a business trip to find his house empty. His wife had left him a message on their answering machine. To make matters worse, Lynn had found another man who would listen to her problems—her boss.

A pastor's every ounce of concern is poured into such calls. Now I (Rich) was being asked to fix a marriage that had been filled with unresolved conflict for years. After several calls, Lynn finally came into my office to talk. Within a few minutes it became evident that for a decade she had been attempting to resolve some major conflicts that Rob saw as only minor.

For the first time in their marriage, Rob began to see things from Lynn's perspective. Now these issues had escalated to a crisis and, while resolution was still possible, it was not probable.

I wish I could report that Rob and Lynn were not Christians, but they are. I wish I could tell you that they confessed their part in the conflict, resolved it, and got back together, but I cannot. I wish they would have seen the gravity of their conflicts early in their marriage and resolved them, but they did not. Lynn kept hoping that Rob would "get a clue" and Rob kept thinking the conflicts would go away. Rob got his wish, but not in the way he had hoped.

When we ignore the need for resolution, we not only rob ourselves of the opportunity of growing, we risk the loss of the relationship and all that goes with it.

When we see conflict for what it is and seek to resolve it using the Bible's wisdom, growth occurs: growth in our own character and growth in the affected relationships. The following story illustrates this principle.

## DIVING IN

Each of you should look not only to your own interests but also to the interest of others (Philippians 2:4).

The sun blistered the back of my neck as I (Marty) watched the gold Steele lure mimic a struggling fingerling inching its way toward the rock where I stood. No strikes yet, but the promise of steelhead moving through the hole drove the adrenaline through my veins. As I studied the current, the lay of the North Santiam, the colors and shades of the water, I felt studied, too. Not by the silver-bodied athletes swimming in the shallows, but by a small boy, shaded by the white-barked birch that drooped like a perfect cast over the rocky bank. There, wide-eyed and with an "I'm gonna be a fisherman too" ear-to-ear grin stood my second-born son, Christopher.

"Kin I come out there on the rock wiff you? Kin I?" his 5-year-old voice pleaded.

"It's too swift out here. You need to stay on the bank."

I wondered if I was being too easy with my three sons. How would I teach them that life should be less about them and more about others—others like me? I reached back for another cast, the sparkle of the gold lure eclipsing every other light—except the twinkle in those eyes. I turned back the pages of my memory. How many times had I stood on various banks of the rivers of the Pacific Northwest hanging on every cast, every skill my dad demonstrated? How many times had I wanted to stand with him out in the wild rapids and dangerous currents?

I struggled.

"I cud jist sit there. I wudn't move." His entreaties carried across the current. I looked down at the gray tackle box near my feet.

*Hmm. He could play with the bobbers and rubber worms,* I reasoned. I tucked my 18-year-old Mitchell 300 into a crack of the rock. "OK. Stay right there," I warned.

Wearing only running shoes, I slid my feet into the frigid current and sloshed over to my son. When I stepped within three feet of the bank, Christopher launched his young frame into my arms, almost slipping through my grip into the icy waters.

"Hey, hey, now wait till I get you on my back" I scolded. "You almost slipped in." His body tensed and I sensed his concern. "It's OK. I'm not upset. Let's just make sure we don't both fall in on our way out." He tightened his grip around my neck, and I knew, instantly, he'd be OK.

"Kin I net him?"

"If we get one," I assured him, doubting whether our father-son duo would send enough casts to have a chance.

I made sure he placed one foot and then the other securely on the rock before I let go of my grip. "You on?"

"Yeah," he cheered, shoving both fists high above his head.

"Just make sure you don't fall in. We have to share this rock, you know." I climbed onto the rock, grabbed the Mitchell, and stood to cast.

"Kin I play with the worms? How come some of 'em are gween? Kin I play with the bobbers, too?" I looked down at his little hand hovering above the waiting toys.

"Does God like to fish? Are you 'fraid of sharks?"

I reached back with the lure and slung it across the river, angling it toward the edge of a pool, when I noticed a small red-and-yellow bobber float past my feet.

"Daddy! Where's the yellow one?" Christopher's frightened voice followed the bobber down stream.

"Chris. I told you to be careful. What were you thinking?

I can't be buying new bobbers every time you lose one."
The fact that I was complaining about something that cost
less than twenty cents slapped me in the face, but I went
on. "Now sit there and play quietly."

His silence drowned the stream as I reached back for
a second cast, and a third, and a fourth. Suddenly I heard
a sickening splash. I turned to see Christopher struggling
in the current, his face filled with fear as he reached for a
large, clear bobber that floated outside his grasp. I slid into
the chill.

Grabbing his shaking arms, I floated a few feet with him,
trying to gain a foothold. Only a few seconds passed before
I pulled him from the current—but it might as well have
been an eternity. "The bobber. Daddy, I got the b-bobber!"
Shaking, he held it toward me as he cried.

I cried, too.

"Chris, Chris. It's alright. I'm so sorry!" I held him to my
chest, hoping my apology would warm his freezing frame
and somehow erase the cold created by my words. I wanted
so much for him to know that bobbers didn't matter, that
steelhead didn't matter, that only he mattered. But, it was
too late. Everything I'd said had proved the opposite.

I carried him to the bank where we sat silently in the sun.
Christopher, so glad that he'd reached the bobber despite
the danger, laughed at the fingerlings swimming near
his feet. I couldn't even hope for the same emotion. Just
moments before I'd been so concerned about his inability to
put the wants of others before his own that I hadn't noticed
my inability to do the same—to demonstrate to my 5-year-
old son what he had, now, so sacrificially demonstrated
to me. As we hurried back toward the campsite wet and
worn, Christopher reached over and squeezed my hand. I
squeezed back.

## OWNING UP

I could have walked away from that experience hoping that Christopher would forget or move on. But somewhere deep inside I knew he couldn't. The conflict I had created in our relationship wasn't a shrugger. This was something I needed to hold close to my heart for a long time. Something I needed to work to reverse. This was my problem to fix. I can't say that the damage is over. Chris is a teenager now and, although he laughs about the story, I know that during the confusing moments most teens experience, it still hurts him. So, I keep on trying to undo the wrong I have done. That's what relationships are all about—each of us developing the willingness to make the necessary sacrifices to redeem whatever we have ruined.

### Huggers: Steps for Identifying Major and Minor Issues

1. Make a list of skills and character traits the individual might gain if you share instead of bear his or her part of the burden.

2. Make a list of the potential damage that could be done if you do not "bear" this burden.

3. Share both lists (#1 first) in a non-threatening environment of the other person's choosing— perhaps over a meal.

4. Ask the other person for his or her "insights" about whether the conflict is minor or major, and accept each "insight" without disagreeing.

Separating the shruggers from the huggers can help us stay focused on the relational conflicts that are ours to solve.

**Changing the Frequency: Keep Track of Conflicts Shrugged**

Each time you shrug off a conflict, make a note in your home or office calendar. In a few months look back at your calendar and thank God for how he resolved the conflict each time you shrugged. Write the solution next to the conflict you shrugged off. This will decrease the frequency of your relational conflicts because it will provide a practical and personal way for you to see that God can fix what you can't.

**BOLD IDEAS**

When a thunderstorm is brewing outside, sometimes the best thing is to come inside, out of the rain.

Solving conflict involves learning to *shrug.*

Failing to shrug can create new problems and delay the maturity that comes from learning to fix our own mistakes.

Whenever we respond to a minor issue in a major way, we undermine our *future* ability to be effective in resolving conflict.

## CHAPTER THREE

# SOLUTION

## CHERISHING DIFFERENCES

*We don't love qualities; we love a person; sometimes by reason
of their defects as well as their qualities.*
—Jacques Maritain

*It is not our purpose to become each other; it is to recognize the other,
to learn to see the other and honor him for what he is.*
—Hermann Hesse

In Dr. Seuss's classic, *Horton Hears a Who*, Horton discovers
that perceived differences shouldn't affect our value as
persons. I (Rich) was twelve when I read *Horton Hears a Who!*
I don't remember where I was or how I came across this
children's book. I do, however, remember the impression
made on me by the words, "A person's a person, no matter
how small."[1]

### VALUING THE PERSON

Some years ago I heard a conference speaker tell a story
about visiting his son and daughter-in-law. As he sat

comfortably on the couch, his 4-year-old grandson ran up to him pleading, "Grandpa, come and look at my room!" The speaker confessed that his first response was to ignore the request. But, instead, he asked himself, "What will my grandson think about *himself,* if I don't see his room?"

He decided that seeing the room was important because responding to the request acknowledged the child's worth as a person. The few moments he spent in that room furnished their relationship for years to come. Why? Because friendship gets up from the couch only when it responds to this truth: "a person's a person no matter how small." Although understanding this principle is the beginning of any successful relationship, it's also a critical part of redeeming relationships damaged by differences.

The first book of the Bible, Genesis, teaches that we were created in the image of an immense and complex God (1:26). Our collective differences express his complex unity. In this sense, whenever we forget to cherish our differences, we forget to cherish his uniqueness. And, we lose out on the pleasures we could derive from our differences. In George Orwell's short story, "A Hanging," a prison inmate echoes a similar concern. As the body of a fellow prisoner sways on the gallows, the inmate whispers, "One mind less, one world less." That's a sobering thought. Forgetting that "a person's a person, no matter how small," can cause us to miss out on the "mind" and the "world" their differences offer us.

## VALUING THE DIFFERENCE

When we face conflicts caused by our differences, it helps to start the resolution process by changing how we think, not only about the value of a person, but about the value of the difference itself. This is especially important because the Bible indicates that God created many of those differences—the same differences we allow to damage our relationships. For example, the Bible says:

> For you created my inmost being; you knit me together in my mother's womb. I praise you because I am fearfully and wonderfully made; your works are wonderful, ... . All the days ordained for me were written in your book before one of them came to be (Psalm 139:13–14).

> The word of the Lord came to me, saying, "Before I formed you in the womb I knew you, before you were born I set you apart; I appointed you as a prophet to the nations (Jeremiah 1:4–5).

Like the psalmist and prophet, we are born with "appointed" differences. Other differences, like habits, are added to our personalities by family, friends and the entertainments we choose. When we work to cherish differences of either kind (those we're born with or those we pick up as we experience life) we reduce the potential for conflict. Most counselors will tell you that, after a few experiences of working through differences, it gets easier. And, happily married couples will tell you that often the differences that seem most divisive are the very differences that draw them closest. Whether our conflicts are related to differences such as how many lattes to buy in a week, how to initiate romance, how to perform a specific task at work, or how to raise children, we can learn to deal with differences.

## TWO KEY QUESTIONS

To write a chapter for a business textbook on how to teach conflict resolution, I (Marty) talked with other professionals and read hundreds of pages about helping employees work through their differences. Those ideas, along with the wisdom in books from the Bible such as Proverbs, helped me develop two simple questions I use to reduce the number and severity of relational conflicts in my life. These same questions are in the material that my wife Linda and I use when we counsel couples.

1. Will spending time and energy on getting the other person to change really be all that profitable? (If that worked, you probably wouldn't be reading this chapter, right?)

2. Is it possible that the difference I'm wrestling with may actually add some positive quality to my life?

We have found that these two questions are a good step-off point for learning to think in a new way about the differences that damage most relationships.

## Go Big or Go Home

Although the phrase "Go big or go home" comes from the sports arena, it also works when thinking about handling conflict. My (Marty's) son Justin used this phrase as the theme for the wing of a men's dorm where he's a Resident Assistant. He thought it might build some motivation, as well as discourage conflict. The idea of going "big" is that motivation and change seem to work best together when we aim high, when we set our sights on the most difficult tasks and "go for it." This principle also holds true for relationships.

One of the most effective ways to change our thinking is to start with the most difficult example of a difference that causes conflict. So, instead of starting with differences like football versus shopping or hunting versus shopping (OK, so I just reminded you that a couple of men are writing this book!), let's "go big." Let's begin with the most difficult difference: How do we cherish someone who can't or won't (yet) accept our differences?

## THE MOST DIFFICULT DIFFERENCE

Eddie and Liz walked into my (Marty's) office at the college one beautiful spring afternoon. The dating couple slumped into the two Windsor chairs next to my desk. Eddie launched right in. "Liz doesn't seem to care about my opinions. We spend more time arguing than anything else." After a half-hour of listing differences and talking about how to handle them, we prayed together, and the two left for the campus dining hall. I asked Eddie to come by the next day.

"So, how did it go at dinner?" I placed a 3x5 card on the corner of the desk. Eddie shook his head, staring at the carpet patterns beneath his feet.

"She doesn't get it. She thinks it's all about *me* not being willing to change for *her*."

"Is it?" I handed him the card and a pen. "I'd like you to write down what you think you'd have to change to make her happy." (My goal was to have him work on one difference at a time.) He paused, picked up the pen and wrote,

"Me."

I chose this example because Eddie's comment demonstrated unusual insight. During our discussions, Eddie began to see that Liz wasn't the kind of person who had any desire to appreciate his differences. That was a crushing blow. But, it was a difference Eddie learned to accept and eventually cherish. Why? Because Liz's intransigence helped Eddie learn to love in a deeper way— with the kind of love that says, "She doesn't *have to* meet me halfway." In a painful yet powerful way, Liz's inability to change gave Eddie a new ability to cherish—an ability he's glad is now part of the man he has become.

I'd like to say that Liz eventually learned to cherish Eddie's differences, but that never happened. In fact, three years later, Eddie married someone else. The most difficult difference to deal with is the one that requires *us* to cherish someone who cannot (or will not) cherish us. Whether it's a coworker, an employer, a family member or a neighbor who can't accept or appreciate our differences, we can learn to cherish theirs. We can, at the very least, allow the conflict to teach us how to love more than "halfway." If we can learn to "go big" with this, the most extreme difference in a relationship, the other conflicts caused by our differences will begin to both disappear and diminish in frequency.

---

**Changing the Frequency: Learning to Cherish the Differences**

Learning to cherish the most difficult difference—a person's inability or reluctance to accept our differences—can help us learn to love in a deeper way. And, because mature love changes our thinking about differences, it will reduce the frequency of the conflicts they cause.

---

## DIFFERENT PERSONALITIES

In the book of Acts, church leaders Paul and Barnabas disagreed over the usefulness of a coworker, John Mark. Barnabas wanted to take John Mark on their next assignment and Paul did not. This disagreement affected their ministries and their relationship because they saw John Mark through the eyes of their different personalities. If these leaders of the New Testament church struggled with personality differences, so will we.

Some of the greatest conflicts we face are over issues of personality. In their book, *Opposites ~~Attract~~ Attack: Turning Your Differences into Opportunities,* Jack and Carole Mayhall list some of the personality differences that create conflict.[2]

- *Differences based on how we think*:
  Factual vs. Intuitive, Logical vs. Relational.

- *Differences based on the way we relate*:
  Introvert vs. Extrovert, Affectionate vs. Reserved.
- *Differences based on the way we talk*:
  Revealer vs. Concealer.
- *Differences based on the way we act*:
  Perfectionist vs. Non-Perfectionist,
  Aggressive vs. Timid.
- *Differences based on the way we look at life*:
  Pessimistic vs. Optimistic.

The list clearly shows the range of personality differences that affect our relationships. We are wired differently—so differently that when we try to communicate, our personalities get in the way. When we try to share our ideas or feelings, we find instead, figuratively speaking, that our calls get dropped, we go over our minutes, or we cross into areas without service. And we don't like it. It frustrates, even infuriates—and then we have it—relational conflict, complete with overage charges!

For years I (Rich) have used the Myers-Briggs Type Indicator to help people reduce the number of conflicts caused by personality differences. I smile each time I read my own composite description.

### Extrovert-Intuitive-Thinker-Perceiving(ENTP)

Quick, ingenious, good at many things. Stimulating company, alert and outspoken. May argue for fun on either side of a question. Resourceful in solving new and challenging problems, but may neglect routine assignments. Apt to turn to one new interest after another. Skillful in finding logical reasons for what they want.

I love the first sentence, "Quick, ingenious, good at many things." If I had my way, it would end there. However, there is more. It starts out well—"stimulating company, alert"—but ends up stepping on my toes. The next line nails me:

"May argue for fun on either side of a question."

I have always been able to see both sides of an issue. It may be one of my strong points. In my youth I would play the "devil's advocate" on an issue. One day, while discussing a matter with my family, I took the opposite side of an issue just for the sake of argument. In the middle of the conversation, my dad stopped and said, "What are you doing, son?"

"Playing the devil's advocate," I smugly responded.

"Son," my dad said, "the devil doesn't need any help from you!"

We all balance strengths and weaknesses. If I park on my strengths and do nothing about my weaknesses, I will continue to experience conflicts with those around me. If they take the same approach, our conflicts increase. I am an extrovert. LouAnna, my wife, tends to be an introvert. When we first started dating, we thought we had found the person of our dreams. I had finally found a woman who would let me talk for the entire date. She would gaze into my eyes, smile and nod as I pontificated about solutions to the problems of the world. Later she confessed that she was drawn to me because she was not expected to talk a lot. She had finally found someone who would carry the conversation and not require much feedback.

I loved this trait, until we married and encountered our first conflict. I think out loud. LouAnna speaks only *after* thinking. When we encountered problems in our relationship, I wanted to talk about it right then! The intensity I projected into the conflict caused Louanna to retreat into silence. The more I demanded responses, the quieter she became. Over the years, we both have moved to the middle. I have learned the value of timing, and she has learned to respond even if she's not as ready as she'd like to be.

When people live together, their differences become pronounced. As the Dean of Students at a Christian college,

I had to encourage many students to resolve conflicts created by differences in personality. For example, when you put an extrovert and an introvert in the same room, conflict will happen.

The introvert goes off to dinner. While she's gone, the extrovert fills the dorm room with people. The introvert returns to find people sitting on her bed and she's offended. The extrovert sees her anger, but does not understand the offense.

## WE NEED EACH OTHER

Our churches, homes, and communities are filled with multiple personalities—it's no wonder our lives seem so schizophrenic some days! I (Rich) have always seen the role of a leader as a facilitator—someone whose goal is to bring the personalities together.

When I began working as a pastor at Valley Bible Church, the thought of our first planning session was noxious to the "free spirits" in our congregation and a breath of fresh air to the "detail lovers." I began with the question, "If we had unlimited resources (financial, building, and human) what could we do for the cause of Jesus Christ?" Immediately, the detail lovers were suspicious. Some even said under their breath, "Not this again!" The visionaries were elated as ideas flowed onto the white-board, but I had to keep reminding the detail-oriented personalities to stop throwing cold water on the dreamers. After a short break, we reconvened and I changed the question.

"What on this list fits our objectives and our resource limitations?" Immediately, those who loved the details came alive. As we continued, I again changed the question to, "In considering the plans that fit our resources, what should we do first?" Both groups of personalities came together as we forged a plan that contained both the dream and the details.

## DIFFERENT PERSPECTIVES

Mature people understand that it's not necessary for everyone to see everything the same way. In fact, the underlying concept taught in the Bible about the spiritual gifts God gives us when we become part of his family is that the church is made up of different members. Those members see ministry from different perspectives.

> Now the body is not made up of one part but of many .... If the whole body were an eye, where would the sense of hearing be? If the whole body were an ear, where would the sense of smell be? But in fact God has arranged the parts in the body, every one of them, just as he wanted them to be ... so that there should be no division in the body, but that its parts should have equal concern for each other (1 Corinthians 12:14–25).

Although Paul is writing about spiritual gifting in Christ's "body" (the Church), his analogy can help us. Among the many truths revealed by Paul are two that fit our discussion: (1) We are tempted to deny the importance of people who are not like us, and (2) Effectiveness and belonging are not based on sharing identical perspectives. The eye has an eye perspective and tends to expect everyone to see what he sees. The ear has the same problem. We all have the tendency to measure others by our perspectives. The following steps can help us change that tendency and communicate effectively when we try to redeem relationships divided by personality differences.

### Step 1: Think "team"

God has made us unique *not* for the purpose of driving each other nuts, but so that we can be stronger. For example, intuitive people need concrete thinkers around to remind them of the details, to inspect and check records, and to edit. Concrete thinkers can also help the intuitive personality remain calm and patient. Concrete thinkers need intuitive dreamers to introduce ingenuity to their solutions, to help them see the possibilities and potentials, and to serve as cheerleaders when projects seem overwhelming.

People who use logic need to work with others who make decisions based on values. They need them to encourage with enthusiasm and to mediate and moderate. People who use their value systems to make decisions need logical thinkers to help analyze and organize their thoughts and to point out problems before they emerge. We need to think "team."

## Step 2: Do an assessment

Do you remember Sheila? In the Introduction we explained how she lost her job because she underestimated the importance of getting along with others. When she told her husband she'd been fired, she could see from the expression on his face that he already knew why.

Tim suggested they see a counselor. The counselor used personality tests to help them see how their perspectives contributed to their conflicts. This new information stimulated Sheila to change the way she treated people. She was still strong-willed, but she became softer around the edges.

Even if you don't take a personality test or see a counselor, you can do an assessment of your personality type and how it affects your perspective in life.

## Step 3: Take control

Third, we need to take control—of ourselves. After all, you are the only person that you *can* control. Normally we concentrate on the people around us. We complain about them and wonder why they are so difficult to get along with. When we blame, we miss the opportunity to change ourselves. It's better to ask, "In what way do I drive *them* nuts?"

There are two problems in life: The one we are facing and our response to it. We may not be able to control the first one, but we can control the second—our response.

*There are two problems in life:*
*the one we are facing and our response to it.*

## Step 4: Give permission

Early in my marriage I (Rich) gave my family and friends permission to tell me how my personality affected them. I thought there would be only a few conversations. However, I found them more frequent than I wanted. Most were on target!

Without permission, all but the boldest will avoid confronting us. One of the first conversations I have with people I work with goes like this: "I know that my personality can be difficult—I'm giving you permission to have any conversation with me you believe will help us be a better team." Most of the time this frees my coworkers to do the same.

## Step 5: Communicate your concern, not just your critique

In my Organizational Communication course I (Marty) teach five principles people can use when personality conflicts arise. These principles come from various journals, experience, and the Bible's books of Proverbs and Galatians.

### Communicating Confrontation

1. **Outline.** Write out what you are going to say and how you are going to act.

2. **Do it privately.** Never remove someone's dignity.

3. **Come alongside—literally.** Approach the person from the side, thereby avoiding the impression of a frontal attack. It is disarming and softens the climate of the confrontation.

4. **Don't be indirect.** Make clear statements about what you expect. Begin your sentences with the word "I" instead of using "you," which is the verbal equivalent of pointing your finger. Don't act as if you're a parent speaking down to a child; avoid using the word "should."

5. **Control your emotions.** Anger adds distance, gentleness creates respect.

## Step 6: Create the right climate

I (Rich) learned the concept of creating the right climate from Dr. John Lange. Asked to teach leadership to a class of officers in the military, John was determined to help them discover the importance of climate. As the class progressed, the students (remember—officers of the military) discovered that Dr. Lange was a caring instructor. He promised he'd never give a pop quiz and even brought donuts to class.

However, the evening he was teaching about conflict, there were no donuts. As the Commander entered the room he smiled at Dr. Lange and cleared his throat. "I want to ask about last week's assignment."

"Commander, last week's assignment was written at the eighth grade reading level. If you need clarification, you don't belong in this class." John was determined to "let them experience the lesson." The Commander, embarrassed, muttered some obscenities and made his way back to his chair.

Next, Dr. Lange indicated that he was going to give a test on the reading material—a test which would comprise fifty percent of their grade. Some tried to remind him that he said that he wouldn't do this, but he merely retorted that he was in charge.

When John stated that "time was up," a colonel was still writing. John walked over to him, yanked his paper from the desk, walked to the garbage can and dropped it in. Then John slowly moved to the board and wrote:

## YOUR LEADERSHIP STYLE CREATES A CLIMATE.

It took the class several minutes to realize they had just experienced the lesson. John had created a harsh, inflexible, and confusing climate, much like a popular model in the military. Does your personality infuse your climate with conflict? Use this chapter (and the rest of this book) to help you change the climate.

### Step 7: Pray about it

We're not breaking new ground to mention that we should pray *before* trying to confront personality problems, but often we forget to do just that. Here's how to pray:

### Praying about Confrontation

1. **Pray for courage.** One of the reasons we don't confront personality problems is because we lack courage. It will still be difficult. But with courage, you can do it.

2. **Pray for an open heart.** When we confront with the idea that we are right, very little resolution occurs. Pray that God will prepare your personality for the other person's.

3. **Pray for wisdom.** In the book of James, we are encouraged to pray for wisdom. It is often the

missing ingredient in our attempts to resolve conflict.

**4. Pray for the above with those involved.** In some settings and with some individuals, this may not always be possible, but—when possible—pray. It sets the tone.


## CHERISHING DIFFERENCES

The following story describes what cherishing differences looks like.

### *The Dress That Wore Her Love*

It was kind of embarrassing and weird. Walking through the Salem Center Mall looking for a formal for my wife felt like trying to get on the right car of an Italian train. The clothing terms seemed like a foreign language, and the few words I did understand, like "clearance" and "70 percent off," didn't exactly put me on the right track.

Linda and I (Marty) had been married eighteen months when an older couple explained to me that buying something like a formal for her would be a major surprise. Since the senior banquet at the college where we worked was that night and Linda had already settled on wearing the same dress she'd worn the previous year, I knew she wouldn't be expecting a new one. Although I enjoyed surprising my wife, what I didn't know was that this shopping trip would uncover an aspect of Linda's life that would surprise me.

"Can I help you?" I should have noticed the smirk on the young sales associate's face as she practically blindsided me at the "70 percent off" rack. I lifted what I thought was the perfect dress from the rack and showed it to her. Since I had only shopped with Linda for Christmas gifts, I really had no idea what styles she liked. So, I went with what I liked—seemed logical enough since she wouldn't be able to see herself in the dress anyway.

"That's a pretty dress and it's a great price. You won't find a better bargain in the whole mall." Her sales pitch sounded great to me, since I had no intention of shopping the "whole mall" anyway. "You'll probably want a few accessories," she continued.

Thirteen minutes later I was back at our apartment.

I bent the metal neck of the hanger so I could hang the dress from the closet door, thinking: *This'll be the first thing she sees when she walks in. Will she be surprised!*

I should probably explain, here, that Linda and I are a bit like the ol' Donny and Marie show: I'm "a little bit country," and she's "a little bit rock n roll." So, you can probably guess what the dress looked like. Yes, it was pink. Not the 1980s west coast kind of pink the college girls occasionally wore. This was the soft, pastel pink that little girls dressed up in for tea parties. And the length? Well, let's just say it was the only formal at the banquet that brushed the floor with sweeping layers of crinoline and lace. To finish off its country, "70 percent off" charm, each sleeve puffed upward from the shoulder like a transparent cloud, and a pink sash tied the back into a perfect and prominent bow. And the accessories the sales associate so appreciatively endorsed? White lace gloves and a matching hat. I pinned the gloves to the sleeves and the hat to the top of the hanger—to complete the stunning visual impact of my purchase. I guess if you were to sum it up using an allusion, this was a *Gone with the Wind* kind of dress—a movie title I should have understood in the imperative.

An hour later, Linda arrived home and raced to the bedroom to get ready for the evening. When she opened the door, she stood stunned. *Yes! Just the reaction I was hoping for*, I thought as I watched her wonder at the depth of my sacrifice and love.

At the banquet I took pictures of her gliding down the spiral staircase and standing beside her girlfriends. I thought of the passage from the Song of Songs "like a lily among the thorns is my darling among the maidens"—so striking was the contrast!

Later that evening as she reached to hang the pink dress at the back of the closet, I reminded her, "Honey, tomorrow's Sunday. You could wear the dress again." She turned toward me and smiled strangely, like a mentor hoping you can understand her next lesson.

"Did you see anyone else in a dress like this tonight?" The rich auburn in her eyes reflected the highlights in her hair.

"Well, of course not, that's why you were so uniquely beauti …" Then it hit me.

She *didn't like* the dress. But, for some reason she'd worn it the whole evening without a single complaint—the lace, the prominent bow and the crinoline beautifully complemented by her constant smile.

My mind wandered through the evening's events. The smiles and gestures of the college girls as Linda walked by. The huddled faculty wives looking her way. I had assumed they were stares of admiration, but Linda knew she'd been the topic of conversation for other reasons.

"Well, why didn't you say something?"

She put her arms around my neck. "Thanks for thinking about me," she whispered. As she slept that evening, I stared at the closet. Somewhere in there hung a dress—a frilly, old-fashioned thing that would forever minister to me the simple freshness of her love.

Each year when I tell this story to my classes, students stop by to see the picture in my office. I always watch with wonder as their initial reactions of laughter, disbelief (and even some respectful ridicule) turn into something more. Something I still struggle to describe.

Each time I watch the transformation, I hope. I hope that these students will meet the kind of person I live with every day. And I hope that on their lonely days, as they walk, through the malls of their memories, they will see what Jesus meant when he said that life is about more than food and clearance racks and clothes—it's about his love, illustrated for us in the everyday sacrifices we make for each other. Sacrifices we make because differences sometimes require them. That's what I see each time I look at that picture—each time I think about the dress that wore her love.

Differences in personality and perspective don't have to divide us. Learning to sacrifice our own perspectives can secure, for others, the depth of our love. We have seen it again and again: cherishing another's differences is truly redemptive.

**Changing the Frequency: Conflicts Caused by Differences**

The following questions can help you reduce the frequency of conflicts caused by differences:

1. What are the aspects of this issue on which we agree?

2. What can I learn from his or her perspective?

3. What aspects of my personality drive him or her nuts, and how can I minimize this distraction?

4. What can I learn from "cherishing" the difference?

**BOLD IDEAS**

When we work to cherish differences, we reduce the potential for conflict.

The most difficult difference to deal with is the one that requires us to cherish someone who cannot (or will not) cherish us.

When people live together, their differences become pronounced.

We all have the tendency to measure others by our perspectives.

When we blame, we miss the opportunity to change ourselves.

The moment you give permission, you are saying the wall has a gate.

Learning to sacrifice our own perspectives can secure, for others, the depth of our love.

CHAPTER FOUR

SOLUTION

# DEALING WITH CRUSHED CHARACTER

*One of the secrets of life is to make stepping stones
out of stumbling blocks.*

—Jack Penn

*Characters live to be noticed.
People with character notice how they live.*

—Nancy Moser

Years ago I (Rich) had the privilege of riding with a police officer. I remember arriving at a "domestic argument" where we saw a blood-covered woman standing in her front yard, holding a knife. I sat in the patrol car thinking she had killed someone. When the officers assessed the situation, however, they discovered that her fingers were nearly lacerated off her left hand. She had bravely saved her life (and her children) by grabbing the blade as her husband thrust it at her chest.

What caused a 40-year-old man to react in such a way? Alcohol? Drugs? No. He was in a rage over the dinner she'd prepared! His wife told the officers that, emotionally, her husband was an explosion waiting to happen. She lived in constant fear.

In his letter to the church in Galatia, the Apostle Paul explains that relational conflict can be caused by "hatred, discord, jealousy, fits of rage, selfish ambition, dissensions, factions and envy" (Galatians 5:20). These kinds of conflicts are different from those caused by differences in personality. So are their solutions. Where our personalities many times define our fit with others, our nature to do wrong is the result of the intrinsic flaw of every human since the Fall. The Bible calls it "sin." Each of us was born with an innate capacity to create *conflict*.

> "You know the story of how Adam landed us in the dilemma we're in—first sin, then death, and no one exempt from either sin or death. That sin disturbed relations with God in everything and everyone ... But Adam, who got us into this, also points ahead to the One [Jesus] who will get us out of it" (Romans 5:12–14, *The Message*).

You may be saying to yourself that stabbing someone is a little extreme. But is it? Our fingers may not require surgery and the police may not show up, but the words we say and our attitudes often leave the same destructive marks on the human heart.

## LEARNING FROM THE LIST

One glance at the morning headlines and immediately we're struck with the drastic impact of damaged character. History reverberates with political leaders, playwrights, and poets who lament the human capacity to do evil. In Fyodor Dostoevksy's classic novel, *Crime and Punishment*, Rodion Romanovich Raskolnikov kills a pawnbroker and her sister in a crime motivated by avarice and greed. Soon after the murders, Raskolnikov's life begins to decay—until he confesses.

*"There are things which a man is afraid to tell even to himself,*
*and every decent man has a number of such things*
*stored away in his mind."*

—Fyodor Dostoevsky

Whether we read literature or the Bible, we soon discover
an emerging list of patterns that damage a person's character.
The Apostle Paul, the church's first missionary, wrote letters
to the churches about conflicts caused by these character
flaws. The list that emerges in Paul's letters remains the
familiar fodder of the world's writers: witchcraft, hatred,
selfish ambition, envy, drunkenness, slander, lying, stealing,
bitterness, rage, sexual immorality, obscenity, coarse joking,
lust, and greed (Colossians 3:5, Ephesians 5:3, Galatians
5:19).

## THE FLESH

Both sides of this kind of relational conflict—those we
cause and those we struggle through—are affected by what
the Bible calls "the flesh." Our flesh feeds on pleasure and
self-satisfaction. This is why it is so easy for the flesh to take
any evidence of quality character in our lives and trash it:
It feeds the appetite and starves relationships. The Apostle
Paul taught that when a person operates in the *flesh,* he or
she invites an open battle with the *Spirit.* This conflict with
the Spirit carries over to the people we live with. To understand the methods of reducing the impact of this kind of
conflict, let's consider a few of the behaviors in Paul's list.

### Sexual sin

Sexual sin refers to all forms of illicit sexual activity. We get
our word "pornography" from the Greek word *porneia.* It
speaks of sexual misconduct ranging from adultery to sex
outside of marriage. Because it is so prevalent, it can be a
major source of relational conflict.

*"Let's pray that the human race never escapes from Earth
to spread its iniquity elsewhere."*

—C. S. Lewis

Alonzo discovered this the hard way. The biggest conflict in their lives occurred in the bedroom over Alonzo's sexual demands on his wife, Lisa.

"Pastor, what Alonzo wants me to do is unnatural and I just don't feel comfortable having that kind of sex with him," Lisa explained through her tears. After talking to Alonzo, it became evident that he was viewing pornographic materials on the internet and using his marriage bed to live out his fantasies. Although our society condones such practices, it condemned his marriage. His only hope was to eliminate this area in his life—to restore, if possible, the character that once attracted Lisa.

Sexual immorality moves through our lives like a metastatic carcinoma. It invades our minds, our speech, our perceptions, our priorities, and every area of our lives. In his poignant instructions to his young protégé, Titus, the Apostle Paul warns,

> To the pure, all things are pure, but to those who are corrupted and do not believe, nothing is pure. In fact, both their minds and consciences are corrupted. They claim to know God, but by their actions they deny him. They are detestable, disobedient and unfit for doing anything good (Romans 1:15–16).

*"Wickedness is always easier than virtue,
for it takes the short cut to everything."*

—Samuel Johnson

We have become an unshockable society. Having been exposed to every kind of indecent behavior in our news and entertainments, we are no longer stunned by what we encounter. Exposure to these shocking activities can create a lust that destroys our sensitivity to the principles and people that should matter most.

## Idolatry

Idolatry can be defined as worshiping something other than the true God. Whatever draws our attention away from God can become an idol. Even important issues can become idols if they absorb our attention and consume our energy. In America, our gods are many. We worship money, power, independence, materialism, work, pleasure, and people. Although it may not overtly demand our attention, idolatry's bony fingers grip our hearts and slowly choke out our affection for the one true God.

Andy is a good example of how something other than God can become an idol, even for one who wishes to be godly. I (Marty) sat in Andy's home as he shared his financial journey. Working hard for everything he got, Andy had achieved a vice-president's position in a large bank. Earning a 6-figure salary with substantial annual bonuses, Andy's life seemed great. As Andy climbed the corporate ladder, however, his family slowly descended, one rung at a time. Andy's original goal was to earn enough money to be able to serve the Lord overseas without needing to raise support, but over the past several years the bony fingers of corporate success began to choke out the Lord, Andy's wife, family, and ministry.

> *"Man's mind is like a store of idolatry and superstition;*
> *so much so that if a man believes his own mind it is certain*
> *that he will forsake God and forge some idol in his own brain."*
> —John Calvin

When I asked Andy what helped him get back on track, his answer surprised me. He explained that one day while conducting business in a private jet, it dawned on him that "money" had become his "god." He realized that his wife and children had watched him change from a man who cared most about them to a man who was consumed by his career. His boss was stunned when they landed and he handed her his resignation. "I want to keep God and my family first," he explained. "This job is just too stimulating for me to be able to do that."

## Pride

You've probably noticed that the list of vices above (from Galatians Chapter 5) does not mention pride. Bible scholars attribute this seeming oversight to the fact that pride comes from the spirit realm rather than our inner struggle with the flesh (*see* 1 Timothy 3:6).

Whether it is in the home, the workplace, or the church, pride (and its attitude of independence) creates relational conflict. King Solomon wrote, "Pride only breeds quarrels, but wisdom is found in those who take advice" (Proverbs 13:10). Although successful resolution requires solutions that benefit everyone involved, the proud seek only solutions that allow them to "win." They find it nearly impossible to believe what most of us know: that *winning* usually involves *losing*. The following steps can help us redeem relationships damaged by pride and independence.

### *Step 1: Ask the right questions*

### Changing the Frequency:
### Detecting Pride and Independence

Sit with a friend you trust and answer the following questions. For the purpose of this activity it's OK to be a little hard on yourself. Look for patterns that show a tendency toward pride (or independence).

- Do you embellish stories about your accomplishments?

- When you are wrong about a matter, are you able to admit it?

- Does pride keep you from sharing your needs with those who can help?

- Do you like to talk about what you own?

- Do you like to talk about how independent you are?

- Do you talk more than you listen in a typical social setting?

- Are you overly concerned about what others think of you?

- Are you seen by others as a "loner"?

- Do you publicly give yourself the credit for your blessings?

- Do you pray about your needs?

- Do you see yourself as the product of hard work rather than God's blessings?

- Are you reluctant to give mature people permission to confront you?

- Are you reluctant to let others have the credit for your success?

- Do you have to have the last word?

If you answered "yes" to two or more questions, you may be struggling with pride.

### Step 2: Practice humility and allow others to serve you

"Live in harmony with one another. Do not be proud, but be willing to associate with people of low position. Do not be conceited" (Romans 12:16).

Humility is not denying our strengths or abilities; it's having an accurate assessment of them. God hates pride (and the relational conflict it creates) enough to bring the proud down. We have a choice. We humble ourselves or God humbles us.

On the night before his crucifixion, Jesus Christ knelt before one of his closest followers, Peter, to wash his feet. Peter initially refused. Like Peter, many of us are good "feet washers," but resist letting anyone wash ours. But, accepting another's love can change the way we love. We become more sensitive, and we listen differently.

### Step 3: Admit your dependence

*"No man is an island, entire of itself;*
*every man is a piece of the continent, a part of the main."*
—John Donne

Independent people have a hard time admitting they need anyone. They ride through life believing the myth of the Lone Ranger (forgetting he had Tonto). John Donne's maxim, "no man is an island" only reminds them that they never liked poetry. We need to get off the island and admit that we need each other.

Though he used to be a "top angel" in God's service, Satan struggled with pride and chose to put himself first, causing his fall from the heavenly position. In a similar way, his struggle becomes our own when we try to go it alone. It damages our character because it casts supernatural shadows over the love of God inside each of us.

### Principles for redeeming relationships damaged by crushed character

If you or someone you know struggles with conflicts stemming from crushed character, the following counsel can help. We've used these principles in various situations to help couples, friends, family members, and coworkers. Although these principles are listed numerically, they are not in chronological order. They are principles you can choose as they fit.

### 1. Make sure it's a pattern, not an incident

Some of us are conflict magnets and magnifiers. We attract every particle of energy-charged conflict that floats too close. Then we take that conflict and blow it out of proportion. We see character flaws that are only *incidents* and reclassify them as *patterns*. Proverbs 25:7–8 warns, "What you have seen with your eyes, do not bring hastily to court." The proverb warns that even obvious signs are often misinterpreted. Verse 8 concludes by saying, "For what will you do in the end if your neighbor puts you to shame?" The character flaw we thought we saw in another, if hastily evaluated, becomes a character flaw in ourselves. This is why the Apostle Paul is careful to point out in his letter to the Christians in the city of Galatia that if we see someone sin we should seek to restore that person "gently," watching our responses so that we do not fall into sin ourselves (Galatians 6:2).

Proverbs 19:11 counsels, "A man's wisdom gives him patience; it is to his glory to overlook an offense." The "glory" part has to do with the kind of gracious person we become when we patiently overlook an offense. I (Marty) found such a person in my wife. When we were first married, I asked Linda how she was able to overlook offenses. (I was referring to offenses that occurred where she worked.) She explained that every time *I* did something that bothered *her*, she did two things. First, she reflected on three things she loves about me. Then, she tried to determine if my behavior was an incident or a pattern. When my students ask me why our first years of marriage weren't that rough, I share this example. They immediately understand. *Patience* and *overlooking an offense* go a long way toward making a relationship work. The following "Changing the Frequency" shows how this principle can help us manage conflicts caused by the flesh.

**Changing the Frequency: Conflicts Caused by Crushed Character**

1. Get to a quiet place and ask God to help you identify the cause of any of the character flaws listed in Colossians 3:5, Ephesians 5:3 or Galatians 5:19. Work on one behavior at a time.

2. Memorize a passage of Scripture that deals with that behavior. (Use the concordance at the back of a Bible.)

3. Write the negative behavior on your calendar—the day it happens. Write every positive behavior from this individual in the same way.

4. At the end of the week, count the number of times positive behaviors *and the negative one* showed up.

5. If it only showed up the one time, follow the same procedure for a month.

6. If it showed up more than once, you may need to confront the person. Begin the conversation by listing his or her positive behaviors. (If you can't find any, get help from a friend who knows the two of you.) Second, show the person the verse you have been memorizing to help you overlook the offense. Finally, show the individual your calendar.

7. Then, invite the individual to read this chapter. Discuss the options given in the chapter (or in other parts of the book) that would help the person change his or her character.

First, use these principles to learn to manage the incidents. If you can't, or if the incidents have become patterns, move on to the next principles.

## 2. Join the divine cooperative

Drs. Cloud and Townsend explain in their book *How People Grow*,

> Many people are confused about the role of the Scriptures in their growth. They sometimes attempt to learn their religion and theology from the Bible, and growth and counseling from psychology. We believe that the Bible and its great doctrine teach the truths and principles people need in order to grow.[1]

The Apostle Paul, in writing to Timothy, states that "All Scripture is God-breathed and is useful for teaching, rebuking, correcting and training ... " (2 Timothy 3:16). The Bible helps us with character because its very design encourages us to make the kinds of changes that produce Christ-likeness—and there is no more attractive character than his.

When I (Marty) was ten, I had an anger problem. In fact, one day I was so angry with my older brother that I hit him in the chin. Unfortunately (or maybe fortunately, since he was bigger), his heels were up against our lawnmower. My fist sent him backward, over the lawnmower, onto the garage floor. I ran for my life!

A few weeks later in Sunday school, the teacher talked about anger (I was sure my brother ratted on me) and told us to memorize Ephesians 4:32. "Be kind and compassionate to one another, forgiving each other, just as in Christ God forgave you." The Holy Spirit hit me with that verse over and over during the next few years. Eventually, the angry moments subsided and turned to forgiveness. So much so, that today, I *never* struggle with anger—now I struggle with lying!

Memorizing Scripture also helps because it joins us with the Holy Spirit. The Apostle Paul introduces this thought. "So I say, live by the Spirit, and you will not gratify the desires of the sinful nature" (Galatians 5:16).Unfortunately, the church has made this process too complicated. Walking by the Spirit means reading the Bible and following it. It's not some mystical massage we force on our brains after minutes of chanting scriptures or repeating choruses. These things can help us pull away from our absorbed styles of living, but without the words of the Spirit (the Bible) we end up massaging a lot of mush. If we focus on the message God has for us through his word, we will be able to live with the energy of the Holy Spirit.

*"It is extraordinary power from God, not talent, that wins the day. It is extraordinary spiritual unction, not extraordinary mental power, that we need."*
—Charles H. Spurgeon

When we read a passage from the Bible, we should ask, "How does God want to apply this passage to *my* life?" When we honestly ask the question, the Holy Spirit focuses our attention on those areas that need adjustment and helps us demonstrate his spiritual "fruit": "love, joy, peace, patience, kindness, goodness, faithfulness, gentleness and self-control" (Galatians 5:22). When this happens, our character changes and we become more enjoyable to be around. But, memorizing Scripture is not the limit of the divine cooperative. We need to exercise wisdom, as well.

Many believers are confused about God's responsibility and theirs. Some years ago I (Rich) met with a young man who struggled with alcohol. As we talked, I asked him what he was doing to solve the problem. He said that he was "praying a lot." He was expecting God to take away the problem without his help. The Apostle Paul discredited this approach.

> Therefore, my dear friends, as you have always obeyed—not only in my presence, but now much more in my absence—continue to work out your salvation with fear and trembling,

for it is God who works in you to will and to act according to his good purpose (Philippians 2:12–13).

Praying that God will remove a drinking problem is like praying that God will remove my credit card debt. There is no doubt that God could answer that prayer, but the odds are that he won't. I will have to work at it by using the character resources God has given me—my self-control!

> *"I know that I'm not yet the person I can be,*
> *but I thank God I'm not the person I used to be."*
> —A Recovering Alcoholic

God could have easily removed the drinking problem, but after months of praying, the young man finally realized God had other plans for his life, so he enrolled in a Christian recovery program. As he began to develop more self-control, his relationships at home significantly improved. (His character eventually drew his wife to Christ.) The Apostle Paul's letter to Timothy, a young pastor, supports the principle of joining the divine cooperative:

In a large house there are articles not only of gold and silver, but also of wood and clay; some are for noble purposes and some for ignoble. If a man cleanses himself from the latter, he will be an instrument for noble purposes, made holy, useful to the Master and prepared to do any good work (2 Timothy 2:20–21).

Do you see it? If we cleanse ourselves (by cleaning up the areas of our life that are our responsibility), we can once again become "an instrument for noble purposes ... useful to the Master ... prepared to do any good work." In most cases our character can be restored—and always it can be improved. We need to join the divine cooperative; we need to acquire a little sweat equity for the soul.

Since self-control is a part of most changes in character, here's a method I (Marty) use within the divine cooperative.

---

### Sweat-Equity for the Soul: Self-Control

For one week, every day:

1. Do something you don't have to and don't like to do (like cleaning the toilet—getting out of bed doesn't count).

2. Don't do something you could do and would like to do (for example: deny yourself a favorite food or beverage).

This will increase your self-control, make your character more attractive to the people around you, and make your life easier for the Holy Spirit to use. The same methods work for other fruit of Spirit (see Galatians 5:22).

---

### 3. Change the model

Recently, on a trip, I (Rich) spoke to Tim, a young man who had been married for only a short time. In our discussion, the topic for this book came up. He stared at his feet for so long I thought he had drifted off in the middle of our conversation. (My pontifications can do that sometimes!) Finally, he responded.

"I used to think families solved conflict by screaming at each other." He explained that one of the biggest problems he had was raising his voice when he and his wife disagreed. Within the first six months, she was tearfully trying to untie the knot.

"I think I am much better now," he confessed.

"What changed?" I asked.

"I asked Cindy's dad how he and my mom-in-law settled issues in their home. He gave me a new model." Many of us have not had healthy models for relational conflict; sometimes all we need is a new one.

### 4. Take the medicine

The medicine is made up of practical ingredients that, when taken together, are used by the Holy Spirit to produce spiritual health. The first two ingredients have already been mentioned.

**Ingredient 1**:  Spend quality time in the Bible.
**Ingredient 2**:  Spend consistent and quality time in prayer.

The next two ingredients are often difficult in our web-accelerated and Porsche-paced culture. However, they are indispensable when we're dealing with crushed character:

**Ingredient 3**:  Spend quality time with other Christians.
**Ingredient 4**:  Spend quality time making a difference.

These four ingredients combine in the life of the Christian believer to produce good character.

The Apostle Paul reminded Pastor Timothy, "Watch your life and doctrine closely. Persevere in them, because if you do so, you will save both yourself and your hearers. (1 Timothy 4:15–16)

> *"To array a man's will against his sickness is the supreme art of medicine."*
> —Henry Ward Beecher

*Spend quality time with other Christians.* We live in a world of fast-food drive-throughs and automatic garage door openers. Although we are exhorted more than twenty times in the New Testament to be involved with other believers, we're more comfortable ordering a meal from our cars, picking it up in our cars, and eating it in our cars. We seldom have to meet even our neighbors face to face, because we don't get out of our cars until the garage door closes behind us.

I (Rich) grew up in a denomination where church attendance was the primary measure of commitment. I saw many who attended every Sunday, but seldom exhibited the Lord's love the rest of the week. Because of them, I thought attendance didn't help a person's character. However, the Apostle Paul stressed to the church at Ephesus that we become mature and more engaged in helping others when we attend church regularly. A quality church changes our character.

***Spend quality time making a difference.*** Jesus said the second commandment is to love our neighbors. Why is this so important? We believe that part of the reason we need to love others is because it gets us past loving ourselves. We leave our world behind for an instant and enter the world of another. Traveling between these worlds helps us heal from the actions of those whose character has been controlled by their flesh, and it also helps us improve our own character.

As the Apostle Paul concluded his letter to his protégé Titus, he explained that "when the kindness and love of God our Savior appeared," it provided motivation for Christians to "devote themselves to doing what is good." Spending quality time making a difference will not only reflect the kindness and love of God, it will help us become more kind and loving. It will change our character.

> This is a trustworthy saying. And I want you to stress these things, so that those who have trusted in God may be careful to devote themselves to doing what is good. These things are excellent and profitable for everyone (Titus 3:8).

Paul believed that people who focus on others by "doing what is good" are a profit to everyone.

## 5. Go public

Usually, when I (Marty) counsel people to share their character struggles with one or two close friends, they look at me like I've just asked them to kiss a pit bull on the lips.

"I'd rather keep this quiet," they'll usually add.

"So would Satan," I remind them.

So many times when we struggle with sin, we want to keep it a secret. We feel shameful enough as it is. But, keeping any sin a secret allows us to continue to play games. The biblical author James reminded the church to "confess your sins to each other and pray for each other so that you may be healed" (5:16).

At times, going public will involve professional counseling. In our battle against our natural urges, we can lose a rational perspective. When this happens, we need to sit down with a trained professional and sort out the problem.

## 6. Mend bridges

If you'll excuse the pun, there's never been "too much water under the bridge" when two people are willing to work on a relationship. Most relationships can be redeemed. Start by apologizing for past behavior, but make sure the apology doesn't have a single word that attempts to justify your behavior—it won't be received as an apology. (Don't ask us how we know.)

Finally, if your damaged character comes from a sin like stealing, go beyond restitution. Make your wrong more than right. Pay back more than you stole. You'll be well on your way to improving your character and redeeming the relationship.

### CRUSHED BY CHARACTER?

So far, we've been talking about what happens when the

flesh crushes our character, but what if you're on the receiving end? The following advice can help.

## Guard yourself

As a good coach will tell you, sometimes you can't develop a good offense until you first improve your defense. The woman we described earlier in this chapter probably wouldn't be alive today had she not taken extreme measures, but her defense (grabbing the knife blade) was an instinctive reaction that barely saved her and her children. Guarding yourself often involves getting out of the harmful environment. She should have guarded her family long before the incident. Following are four ways to improve your defense.

### 1. Predict and plan

Charles was a victim of jealousy. At every company meeting, Sara picked at the connotation of his words and challenged his assumptions. Charles tried confronting, but Sara argued better. He ended up looking less intelligent and feeling less human.

By the time I (Marty) met with him, he was considering another job. I talked Charles through the principles above, reminding him that Sara's character would eventually show itself. We explored the book of Proverbs together and one proverb jumped out at Charles, "a gentle answer turns away wrath" (15:1). Since he had observed Sara's behavior, Charles was able to predict two scenarios that could occur in the next meeting. Charles wrote out the "gentle answers" he wanted to use in each scenario and practically memorized them (including his tone of voice). The next day, when Sara started her usual attack, Charles responded gently, protecting himself from the frustration he usually felt in her presence. The rest of Charles' team was impressed, as Sara's jealousy became obvious. Charles eventually won the battle by predicting possible scenarios, searching the Scriptures, and planning proper responses.

## 2. Ask for wisdom

*"The function of wisdom is to discriminate between good and evil."*
— Cicero

In the biblical book bearing his name, James reminds us that wisdom from heaven "is first of all pure; then peace loving, considerate, submissive, full of mercy and good fruit, impartial and sincere" (James 3:17). If the wisdom you are reading is from a source other than the Bible, make sure it's pure, peace loving, considerate, submissive, full of mercy and good fruit, impartial and sincere. If not, it isn't wisdom, so don't use it.

## 3. Set boundaries

**boundary:** something (as a line, point, or plane) that indicates or fixes a limit or extent
—Merriam-Webster's Collegiate Dictionary

Drs. Townsend and Cloud popularized the notion of setting boundaries in their book by the same title. I (Rich) remember when several of my hospital colleagues were taking a break in the lounge and one of the ER doctors came screaming in, ranting about the "stupid rule" that required a doctor to check out blood before it could be used. Sandy, the blood bank supervisor, interrupted him, "You may be able to act this way in your department, but in the lab, we are civil with each other." Immediately the doctor stopped, took the blood, and left. He never crossed that boundary again.

## 4. Check the timing

When our cars start running like garbage trucks, one of the things we usually have checked is the timing. The same should be true for our relationships. Most people in the throes of character-damaging behaviors are not remotely interested in discussing how their behavior affects us. So read the temperature gauge. When it goes up, turn off your engine and check your timing. Use the next several minutes to prayerfully prepare what you need to say. King Solomon reminds us "how good is a timely word" (Proverbs 15:23). Checking the timing can help your relationship run smoothly again.

Like Dr. Jekyll and his alter ego, Mr. Hyde, it doesn't take much to move us toward unkind words or selfish responses. These aspects of the flesh are already inside, just waiting for someone to awaken their destructive forces. The resulting character damages our relationships. But, there is hope. They can be redeemed.

---

### Crushed Character FAQs

Q. If I am struggling with habits of the flesh, where do I begin to restore my character?

A. Read back through your journal and compare the events with the fruit of the Spirit in Galatians Chapter 5. Then ask a mature friend for candid responses to your ideas about the relationships between the events and the fruit of the Spirit.

Q. What happens if I confess my problem to someone and they walk away from the relationship?

A. The irony here is that, when we pretend to be perfect, our friends end up valuing someone who doesn't exist. Besides, you'll be surprised at how many will accept you.

Q. I can't afford professional help. What do I do?

A. Start with your local church. There are public services and programs available at no cost. A church can point these out.

**BOLD IDEAS**

Although successful resolution requires solutions that benefit everyone involved, the proud seek only solutions that allow them to "win."

We have become an unshockable society.

Humility is not denying our strengths or abilities; it's having an accurate assessment of them.

Independent people have a hard time admitting they need anyone.

There is no more attractive character than his.

Many believers are confused about God's responsibility and theirs.

Part of the reason we need to love others is because it gets us past loving ourselves.

Most relationships can be redeemed.

Guarding yourself often involves getting out of the harmful environment.

Many of us have not had healthy models for relational conflict; sometimes all we need is a new one.

Sometimes you can't develop a good offense until you first improve your defense.

Read the temperature gauge.

When we pretend to be perfect, our friends end up valuing someone who doesn't exist.

## CHAPTER FIVE

S O L U T I O N

# EDITING EXPECTATIONS

It stunned the critics. Dubbed as a low-budget, small-town documentary, it was expected to fizzle in the theaters. But they were wrong. *October Sky*, a movie based on events in the life of Homer Hickam, a NASA engineer, rocketed up the charts. The story of how four friends rise above the community *expectations* that tried to bury their dreams in the coal mines of West Virginia orbited close to home. But these were not the only expectations viewers identified with.

Throughout the movie, Homer struggles with the expectations of a father who wants him to give up his dreams and join him in the coal mine. When his dad finally relents and tells Homer he can follow in the footsteps of his "rocket science hero, Dr. Von Braun," Homer replies, "Dr. Von Braun's a great scientist, but he isn't my hero."

This powerful declaration from a son who appreciated his father despite the agonizing expectations he placed on him resonated with audiences. Why? Because Homer somehow found the strength to survive the burden most of us bear at one time or another—the burden of expectations.

Whether at work, school, or home, expectations constantly remind us of our failures. The conflicts they create drive us away—but only as far as our jobs, our geography or our family relationships allow. Sometimes we can't just shrug and walk away. We're stuck with the pressure.

*"To free us from the expectations of others, to give us back to ourselves—there lies the great, singular power of self-respect."*
—Joan Didion

## EXPECTING EXPECTATIONS

I (Rich) was blindsided. After the first month of working for a new boss, I was summoned to a late Friday afternoon meeting. My boss, an avid golfer, was rarely found in the office on Friday afternoons, so I knew something was up. My worst fears were realized when I heard him say, "I'm not happy with your performance."

I was managing a department of the hospital and thought I was doing a great job. But, as he spoke, I felt like I was having one of those "out of body" experiences you see in the movies. I was floating somewhere between "but I know what I'm doing" and his eulogy for my hospital career. Then I saw this bright light. Actually, it suddenly dawned on me that he was criticizing me for mistakes that weren't mine. He had neglected to read my job description. I pried my limp body off the floor and calmly explained the situation: People in my position at other hospitals had roles different from mine. Later that afternoon, after reading the job description, his perception changed.

My job had nearly become a victim of incorrect expectations. Each of us carries a list that defines acceptable performance in a relationship. Because they are part of us, they aren't easy to peel away. That's why we need to learn to expect expectations. And to recognize those that are not ours to carry.

Each of us has expectations that help us formulate and identify satisfaction in our relationships. Bosses have lists for employees; employees have lists for their bosses; friends carry lists for each other, as do husbands for wives and wives for husbands. Expectations come from experiences, friends, people we admire or dislike, value systems, families, cultures, churches, the Bible, and our entertainment choices. Every relationship is in some way governed by expectations.

*"Our environment, the world in which we live and work, is a mirror of our attitudes and expectations."*
—Earl Nightingale

## GRATING EXPECTATIONS

Goethe stated, "Treat a man as he is, he will remain so. Treat a man the way he can be and ought to be, and he will become as he can be and should be." There are some expectations that work in our behalf. I (Rich) grew up with a dad who expected me to succeed, and his concept of success meant being a person of integrity. Expectations like my dad's normally do not create conflict, unless we don't want to grow. It's the unrealistic and hidden expectations that grate our relationships.

### Expectations explode minor issues

If putting the cap on the toothpaste is important to us, then each day we find the tube without the lid fastened, the expectation moves closer to being of primary importance— even though, logically, it isn't. When the unmet expectation reaches the top of our list of expectations, divorce is a toothbrush away!

### Expectations put us in a parental role

Whenever the other person doesn't comply with our list of

expectations, we find ourselves using parental language, "If you had done _____, this would never have happened." This makes the people around us feel like teenagers again (and those are years most of us don't want to relive).

*"Our desires always disappoint us;*
*for though we meet with something that gives us satisfaction,*
*yet it never thoroughly answers our expectation."*
—Elbert Hubbard

## Expectations reduce the relationship to a performance

"For better or for worse ... ." Most couples mean these vows—until the "worse" part includes living with unmet expectations. When this happens, we stop ice dancing to the careful choreography the other person created. We slip and slide our way through the routine, but we don't measure up. The relationship becomes a performance, a routine, not the combination of planned and spontaneous elements God wanted us to cut up the ice with. We begin to feel loved only for saying and doing the right things—not for being the right person.

## Expectations create high-maintenance relationships

High-maintenance relationships could be defined as those that require constant attention and energy to attain what should feel relaxed and natural. I (Marty) could have asked my wife, Linda, to write this section. Most of our early conflicts resulted from my unrealistic expectations.

One Saturday morning I invited Linda to help me replace the clutch in our Datsun B210. After jacking up the car and setting it on stands, I rested the transmission on my brand new hydraulic floor jack and slid under the car. As I loosened the last bolt from the housing, I asked Linda to lower the floor jack so that I could carefully slide the transmission out of the way. The next thing I knew, the housing was in the middle of my chest! I yelled, "Raise the jack." Linda began pumping the handle frantically. The transmission didn't budge. The only thing that moved was hydraulic fluid squirting out the jack's valve each time she pumped the handle. Thinking that I was dying under the car, she broke into tears.

Although she laughs about it now, I should never have put her in that situation. She'd never worked on a car. She'd never used a floor jack. The emotional conflict I created came from my unrealistic expectations.

## Expectations make it impossible to please

Have you ever met someone who immediately decided you were his or her best friend? You know the type: They call or email, and if you don't reply, they ask if something's wrong. They show up unannounced. Their unrealistic ideas about friendship make it impossible to please them. The resulting hurt creates conflict that is hard to resolve.

### REDEEMING RELATIONSHIPS DAMAGED BY EXPECTATIONS

Redeeming relationships damaged by expectations involves understanding the differences between hidden and unrealistic expectations. Many professional counselors believe that most relational conflict caused by expectations disappears when hidden expectations are brought out into the open, unless the hidden expectations are also unrealistic.[1] Unrealistic expectations are the most difficult to resolve because the cause is often a part of the offender's personality—usually something like perfectionism. We'll explain how to reduce the frequency of hidden expectations first.

*"We love to expect, and when expectation is either disappointed or gratified, we want to be again expecting."*

—Samuel Johnson

### Shelving expectations

In 1970, I (Rich) was in seminary, worked full time at a local hospital, and spoke at various churches on the weekends. LouAnna was home each day with our newborn and a two-year-old. She saw our Saturdays as opportunities to become reacquainted and make improvements on our love nest. I longed for time to study and sleep. We each had a hidden list of expectations and resented each other when our expectations were not met. The following "shelves incident" drew our attention to the problem.

One Saturday morning we were standing in our garage surveying the mess that had slowly pushed our cars onto the driveway. We looked across the street at our neighbor's garage. I noticed their nice cars. LouAnna noticed their nice garage.

"Look at the shelves *they* have!"

I acknowledged that *they* had shelves, stumbled back into the house and subtracted "clean the garage" from my Saturday "to do" list. While I subtracted, LouAnna added "attractive shelving" to her list. That morning her list looked like this:

1. Spends time with me and the kids
2. Stays on his diet
3. Stays on his diet
25. Builds shelves

Two weeks later, we visited the local hardware store. For some reason we stopped in front of the shelving display. Again, LouAnna mentioned how "*nice* it would be to have shelves in our garage." I thought that working full time, attending seminary, and ministering on the weekends were "*nice*" things, too. Shelves were not on any list that I knew about. At this point, her list looked like this:

1. Spends time with me and the kids
2. Stays on his diet
3. Stays on his diet
8. Builds shelves

In two weeks the shelves had moved from #25 to #8!

Several weeks went by and we found ourselves again standing on an even smaller patch of garage floor. LouAnna said, "When are you going to get *us* those shelves?"

"Shelves?" I sensed tension. The list now read,

1. Builds shelves
2. Builds shelves now!
3. Spends time with me and the kids
4. Stays on his diet

You should see the shelves in our garage!

Excuse the pun, but it's important to learn to "shelve" our expectations, to replace them with a deeper understanding of the needs of the other people involved. The Apostle Paul told the church at Philippi, "Each of you should look not only to your own interests, but also to the interests of others" (Philippians 2:4). The principle of looking to each other's interests can help us avoid *expecting* our family, friends, and coworkers to meet our own. The first step is getting our list (and theirs) out in the open.

### Step 1: Hand over the list

> "*Life is so constructed, that the event does not, cannot, will not, match the expectation.*"
> —Charlotte Bronte

The minute that I (Rich) produced my job description, the relationship with my new boss improved. The change in our relationship was the result of handing over the list—of getting the expectations out in the open. When you hand it over, the discussion needs to focus on the list rather than the reasons behind the list. Family therapist Paul Coleman suggests that rehearsing specific phrases can help us convey our concerns in a tender and honest manner.[2] When handing over the list, the conversation could go something like:

> I value you and want to improve our relationship. I believe that we may be in conflict over what we expect from each other. If we could write down our expectations, it would allow us to examine them in a nonthreatening way.

*"Before you have a misunderstanding, get an understanding."*
—Richard Davis

### Step 2: Prioritize the list

The "shelving incident" forced LouAnna and me to hand over our lists. We discovered that she was unaware of some of my expectations and I was unaware of hers. We prioritized our lists and decided we would focus on the important issues and work on the others when time allowed. Prioritizing is easier if we remember a few guidelines:

- First list, then define.

- Be clear and avoid emotional statements. "Make the bed and pick up your clothes" is better than "Clean your pigsty of a room now!" For a teen, the second statement could elicit a defense mechanism that could push the individual into the arms and advice of her friends.

- Move character qualities such as gentleness and integrity to the top of the list. Unfortunately, we often trade these character qualities for clean rooms (see Chapter 4). It's important to edit our expectations to include what matters most.

### Step 3: Compare the lists to Scripture

Compare each item in the list with passages from the Bible. The best way to do this is to use a Bible concordance to look up key words in your list. Ask the following questions about each item:

- "Does the Bible support the level of importance I ascribe to this item?"

- "Does the Bible put the item in the same place on the list as I do?"

- "Will my list help grow the fruit of the Spirit in my life?" (see Galatians 5:22)

If the answer to any of these is "no," you'll need to change your list so that the items line up with what God says is most important in our relationships.

The list should be prioritized with the most important item listed first and so on until the list has five or so items. Too many items confuse the conversation and prolong solutions, yet a list with only a few items will probably hide something important.

Concentrate on listing items that are intrinsically important. Items like, "clean the room," should be placed after items like, "when under duress, speak to each other with kindness." "Clean the room" is a task; "kindness" is a character quality (*see* Ephesians 4:32). If either of you is easily distracted, try following an agenda during this meeting.

### Step 4: Guard the lists

These lists are confidential and should be seen only by the people making them. If confidentiality is not guaranteed, the lists will not be honest. Also, the list should not be used to respond to recent frictions or frustrations. It should focus on character.

*"What we see depends mainly on what we look for."*
—John Lubbock

### Step 5: Pray through the lists

James wrote that in the middle of our trials we can pray for wisdom and God will give us wisdom abundantly and without accusing us (James 1:5). We also need to ask God to mold the hearts involved—theirs and ours. Before you pray together, reaffirm your belief that having shared expectations will enhance the relationship. Pray in a neutral place, not in a home, bedroom, office, car, or any place either party claims sole rights to. When the meeting place is public, people usually keep their voices at a respectful level. It should also be a place where you can sit for an extended period of time.

### Step 6: Construct a new list

The beginning should emphasize fact finding. "I found it interesting that you included _____ on your list. How is this important to you? How is this important to us?" Beginning this way allows the meeting to start without confrontation. Focus your energies on understanding what the other is saying rather than on trying to get him or her to understand what you are saying. Don't try to "sell" your list.

*"The little that is completed, vanishes from the sight of the one who looks forward to what is still to do."*
—Johann Wolfgang von Goethe

When the first meeting is finished, review what you have discovered. Set the next meeting time and reaffirm this process. Agree with each other that this new list will become the "mission statement" of your relationship.

### Step 7. Draw the line

The line is the barrier that discourages expectations below it from moving to the top of the list. Everything above the line formulates the important issues we agree to work on (see the following section on "unrealistic expectations" for how to begin). At this point, agree that items below the line will not affect the relationship. Remember, you should show patience and deference, but you cannot let someone's list govern your life. You must draw the line.

> *"I'm not in this world to live up to your expectations*
> *and you're not in this world to live up to mine."*
>
> —Bruce Lee

### Step 8: Periodically review the list

Right after a birthday or holiday are good times to review these lists. (You'll begin to associate that day with the review of your expectations.) Remember, success is never guaranteed but—should we decide to do nothing—failure is ... Reviewing your list will help you reduce the frequency of conflicts caused by expectations.

---

### Changing the Frequency: Hidden Expectations

1. Sit down together and list the expectations you "feel" are being placed on you and what you expect from your partner (spouse, friend, child, parent, boss, etc.).

2. Prioritize the items in the lists.

3. Ask them to go through the same exercise. Use an agenda.

4. Share your written lists without discussing any items.

5. Meet again to discuss which items are most and least important.

6. Check to see that the lists reflect what the Bible says is important.

7. Draw a line across the list. Those items above the line must be accomplished in a timely fashion to the satisfaction of the partner; those items below the line are icing on the cake but not essential. Agree not to add to the list until both people are satisfied.

8. Meet weekly to review the lists.

## UNREALISTIC EXPECTATIONS

When we hand over our lists, we sometimes find that they contain unrealistic goals and desires. Unrealistic expectations are difficult to change because most of them come from perfectionists—people who are perfect at arguing, at manipulating, at everything except redeeming relationships. Their fear of being found out (yes, most of them realize they aren't perfect) short circuits their kindness. All their anxiety and angst is directed at their closest friends (the people they feel most relaxed around), creating fully charged conflict.

So what can we do to redeem these relationships? Since conflicts caused by unrealistic expectations won't diminish by handing over the list, the best place to start is to take our focus off our own pain. Although this may appear counterproductive, focusing on *their* pain will change the frequency of conflicts created by their unrealistic expectations. Here's how:

### Give gifts within gifts

My (Marty's) mother-in-law is no fool. She served on the mission field in Cuba and can read people like a Cuban cookbook. When our first son was born, she gave Linda and me a poem in a powder blue frame that matched the nursery. This was part of her carefully crafted plot (which she completely denies). She knew that I'd have to stare at it every night while rocking Justin to sleep:

> *Cleaning and scrubbing can wait 'til tomorrow,*
> *For babies grow up we've learned to our sorrow.*
> *So quiet down cobwebs, dust go to sleep,*
> *I'm rocking my baby, and babies don't keep.*
> —Author unknown

I still remember every detail of that framed poem. Why? Because it opposed things my perfectionistic personality applauded. Besides, I knew that the cute little rhyme, when applied to my life, said something more like, "Marty, you have a problem with perfectionism and it's going to ruin my grandson, so knock it off." Now mom would never have said it that way, but that's how it came through—loud and clear.

Mom took the time to help me see that having "a place for everything and everything in its place" wasn't as important as having a prominent place in my heart for my first-born son. Today my son is one of my best friends, and I am indebted to my mother-in-law for her gift within a gift.

## Encourage their failures

Every year when the freshmen take their seats in my (Marty's) speech classes (yep, now you can really hate me), it's fairly easy for me to spot the perfectionists. Their clothes and hair are perfect, they sit close to the front, and they've already created a class document on their laptops by the time I walk in. Most of them are well adjusted and aware of the curse they carry, but some are oblivious and frightened; speech classes aren't safe places for perfectionists—the mistakes are far too public!

Before the first speeches, we discuss speech anxiety and failure. I remind the students that failure is a helpful part of life. I try to encourage them by promising an extra point for every risk they take—even the ones they fail at. Then I quote John Fischer:

> *Losin' is winnin' if it turns you around*
> *It all looks clearer when you're close to the ground*
> *When you know you're lost then you can be found,*
> *And you walk out a winner.*[3]

Still, during the first speeches many of the "normal" students are puzzled by the shaking hands and trembling voices of the star athletes and movie star lookalikes.

"Why would someone who's so perfect be so nervous?" they ask after class. That's when I explain that perfectionists struggle with failure, with not being liked, with being criticized in the same way they criticize others.

I remind these students to tell the perfectionists how much their shaking hands and trembling voices authenticated their desire to do well or demonstrated the importance of the topic, that it made them more approachable, that shared failures are one of the foods of friendship.

## Pray for their pain

When a perfectionist wounds us with questions such as, "Why can't you be more like _____?" or "Why are you so inefficient?" or "Why are your kids so _____?" try to move beyond your pain.

These are the walking wounded you're listening to. Their opinions should do little more than call you to prayer on their behalf. Here's what the perfectionist really means:

- "Why can't you be more like _____?" really means, "Pray for me. I don't like myself."

- "Why are you so inefficient?" really means, "Pray that I will find contentment in the midst of my own inabilities."

- "Why are your kids so _____?" really means, "I can't do this parent thing. Pray that my kids will end up healthy and well adjusted."

The list goes on. If you can learn to see the pain beyond yours, you won't solve their problem, but you will reduce the frequency of the conflicts you experience.

## Edit the Expectations

Phil Collins' song, "Two Worlds," in Disney's *Tarzan* movie told us to put our faith in what we most believe in, and that two worlds can become one family.

So our culture tried to make the opposing expectations that "most believe" into "one family." We aligned our expectations with the tolerance crowd, but became disillusioned when we watched their preachers become intolerant of those less tolerant than themselves.

We believe that counseling people to believe they're all doing the right thing, when those right things oppose each other, creates a damaging dichotomy. Because of this, the person seeking help with relational conflict seldom finds any. It may be culturally acceptable to say that no one set of expectations is better than another, but it never plays out. It's unrealistic.

Our Creator created principles that can heal the damage produced by such unrealistic expectations, but he did this by outlining expectations of his own. The Bible shares these with us. We recommend that people start with reading Proverbs and Ephesians. These two books can help us edit the unrealistic expectations of the people who are causing relational conflict in our lives. Here's how:

As you encounter expectations that seem unrealistic, use the concordance at the back of your Bible to look up the words that are related to the expectation. If, for instance, a friend wants you to meet her needs 24/7, you could look up the word "need" in your concordance. It would point you to passages such as Ephesians 4:29 where the Apostle Paul reminds us to "build others up according to their needs" (her point) but adds "that it may benefit those who listen." Your 24/7 availability certainly will not "benefit" her in the long run. The passage helps you use God's style guide to edit her unrealistic expectation.

**Changing the Frequency:**
**Conflicts Caused by Unrealistic Expectations**

### 1. Give gifts within gifts

Movies or articles about sports legends or poems that picture the damage that perfectionism creates can subtly encourage growth. During your reading or movie viewing, keep your eyes open for examples of conflicts caused by perfectionists.

### 2. Encourage their failures

When perfectionists make a mistake, remind them how human it makes them, how much more approachable they are, how helpful it is for them to allow others the privilege of helping them. Hearing this from you will remind them that there is some good in every failure. Sometimes a note saying the same can achieve a similar result.

### 3. Pray for their pain (in their presence)

Praying for the pain that motivates their criticism and the resulting conflict will help them toward understanding why they say and do things that hurt you and others.

### 4. Edit expectations

Use the concordance at the back of your Bible to help you edit the unrealistic expectations people place on you.

*"If you accept the expectations of others, especially negative ones, then you never change the outcome."*
—Michael Jordan

We believe that hidden and unrealistic expectations damage more relationships today than ever before. And, unfortunately, a postmodern mindset that says there are no right or wrong expectations will only encourage this trend. However, those of us who trust the wisdom of the Scriptures can reduce the frequency of these conflicts by sharing our hidden expectations and editing the unrealistic ones.

Mr. Hickam redeemed his relationship with his son, Homer, when he let go of his expectations. Instead of burying Homer's dreams with his own in the coal mines of West Virginia, he encouraged Homer to reach for the moon—which is exactly where Homer's efforts in NASA landed mankind two decades later. Our resolutions may not orbit the silver screen in a movie like *October Sky*, but they will redeem our relationships and honor all of heaven. And maybe, just maybe, our willingness to understand the expectations of another human being will create in us the character of a hero.

**BOLD IDEAS**

Shared failures are one of the foods of friendship.

Every relationship we have is in some way governed by expectations.

When you hand over your list, you help others understand your heart.

God will give us wisdom abundantly and without accusing us.

Timing is the essence of resolving a conflict.

Success is never guaranteed, but—should we decide to do nothing—failure is.

CHAPTER SIX

S O L U T I O N

# Dealing with Immaturity

*Basically my wife was immature.*
*I'd be at home in the bath and she'd come in and sink my boats.*
—Woody Allen

> We proclaim him, admonishing and teaching everyone with all
> wisdom, so that we may present everyone perfect [mature] in
> Christ (Colossians 1:28).

"Move over, idiot!"

If you want to test a person's level of maturity, drive from Vallejo, California to San Francisco with him. I (Rich) took such a drive with a friend (we'll call him John) whom I had perceived as mature. John moved the steering wheel with the precision of a race car driver. Yelling while glaring down other drivers, the John behind the wheel was a person I'd never seen before. I felt like I was in the Twilight Zone. One moment John was the old John, laughing and enjoying our fellowship; the next he was road rage personified. In the past, I had heard "rumors" about how John's temper created high turnover at the new coffee shop he'd opened. Because of John's usual demeanor, I'd dismissed these concerns as "overreactions." Had I been that wrong?

*"Maturity is the ability to think, speak and act your feelings within the bounds of dignity. The measure of your maturity is how spiritual you become during the midst of your frustrations."*
—Samuel Ullman

## Maturity Matters

Immaturity is different from other causes of conflict: it influences how we see every aspect of the world around us. Like social and spiritual cataracts, immaturity blurs and blinds our perceptions. It isn't something we acquire from our inner struggles with crushed character (see Chapter 4); it's the lack of understanding and willpower we demonstrate when we don't continue those struggles. For instance, John was blind to his behavior. He only had a vague idea of how it affected the people around him—until Cherie pointed it out in a note that wrecked John's world.

> For four years I have put up with your yelling, whining, and complaining. You keep saying you'll try harder, but I don't see any change. I'm sorry, but I'm leaving.
>
> *—Cherie*

Now John sat in my car reading the note aloud as we made our way to Cherie's attorney's office.

The meeting was short. Cherie wanted to see obvious "evidence of consistent change" in John's level of maturity. It was a "take it or I'm leaving you" proposition. John was convincingly reminded that maturity matters.

If you're in a relationship with someone whose immaturity has crushed your spirit or diminished your view of your place in this world, this chapter can help you heal. If you are an individual who, figuratively speaking, has been handed papers that read "you're immature," this chapter can help you, too. Otherwise, you're probably reading this chapter because some event or someone has convinced you, too, that maturity matters.

## CHANGE OR GROW UP!

In his book *I Really Want To Change ... So Help Me God,* James MacDonald contrasts growth and change. It is an important distinction. We mistakenly believe that if given enough time we will grow out of our immaturities. This is not true. Some have carried their immaturities to the grave. Growth involves long term, subtle adjustments. Change is something that is needed immediately.[1]

When I (Marty) started coaching t-ball, I was one of those self-appointed policy police. I remember marching across a field one beautiful Saturday afternoon and chewing out the other team's coach for failing to play his bench. I was too immature to see that my limited view of the world was affecting not only the coach, but the parents sitting behind him. That night I talked with my family about the event. I asked them to pray for me and to see if they could figure out a way to help me relax and enjoy the game despite the occasional rule violations. My wife, Linda, volunteered (bless her heart) to be the one to remind me. The *change* was immediate. It took some time, however, for me to bench the immaturity.

Believing people will "just grow out of" immaturity is the fulcrum of parenting philosophy for many today. We overlook behavior in our kids that we know is destructive and immature. We do so under the misguided belief that they will just "grow out of it." While we do grow out of most of our immaturity, even that process involves some outside event or person. Often parents hope church programs and special school curriculums will produce both change and growth. However, God has designed the home and the role of the parent to provide the events that take children to the next level.

I (Rich) remember acting like a jerk when I was a kid. I'd mock Dad's instructions, repeating his words under my breath as he walked away. ("Clean up your room, Richard." You know the tone.) My Dad often reminded me that such behavior was not acceptable and that my antics, if they continued, would bring painful consequences. One time after he shared some of those painful consequences, I accused him of not being my friend.

"Son," he said, "you have plenty of friends, you have only one father." It was not pleasant confronting a strong-willed son, but my dad believed it was his calling. Early in John's life, people, including his parents, missed opportunities to help him change. They could have made a difference, but didn't. As a result, John sat in an attorney's office.

If you have ever been with children, you realize they are self-absorbed because they are at the center of their own worlds. This is normal for a child. It is abnormal for an adult. Children think in simple terms that place them and their pleasure at the center of almost every action and decision. Their thinking is clouded by an inability to reason as an adult. Instead of being rational, they are irrational. They are highly emotional and can erupt at the slightest provocation.

## PUTTING AWAY CHILDISH THINGS

I (Rich) discovered this when I returned home after my first year of college. Some of my high school buddies wanted to get together one evening to "catch-up" with each other. Half way into the evening, I realized that some had matured, but many were limited to talking about the same things they did in high school. Something much more serious than a year had passed between us.

College was a growing experience for me. As a result, I talked, thought, and reasoned differently. I wasn't better than my friends, but we had less in common. I wanted something more in our conversations than an assessment of the new cars at the dealerships and the new "babes" in the neighborhood.

In his first letter to the church in Corinth, the Apostle Paul reminded his readers that, when he was a child, he talked, thought and reasoned like a child, and that when he grew up, he put "childish ways" behind him (1 Corinthians 13:11). It's this act of putting that is so difficult. How does a person learn to put away childish things?

## The Art of Putting and Pushing

Steven Covey in his book, *The 7 Habits of Highly Effective People,* contrasts the animal's response to stimuli with the human's.[2] He concludes that the animal can only react, but humans have been given a pause button which can be pushed to suspend a response to stimuli. One of the characteristics of the immature is that they rarely hit the button. Without any effort given to editing their thoughts, they say what's on their minds. Not only does this penchant for childish conversation create conflict, it exacerbates it.

### Learning to shift

After years of observing college students, we believe movement from immaturity to maturity is characterized by, but not limited to, several noteworthy shifts. These can be difficult shifts—like the shifts you learned to make when you first got behind the wheel of a car with a manual transmission.

- A shift from dependence and independence to interdependence.
- A shift from egocentricity to others-centricity.

- A shift from passivity to proactivity.

- A shift from pleasure-centeredness to purpose-centeredness.

- A shift from the acquisition to the application of knowledge.

### Shifting from dependence and independence to interdependence

When men or women start maturing, they naturally move from being dependent to being independent. As they continue to mature, they discover an appreciation of the community around them and become *interdependent.* The immature, however, are often either dependent on others for their needs or so independent that they become islands in the social sea.

Moving to adulthood requires growth in the area of interdependence. The following passages from the Bible indicate that interdependence is something God created for our benefit.

- Accept one another (Romans 15:7).

- Admonish one another (Romans 5:14; Colossians 3:16).

- Be concerned for one another (Hebrews 10:24).

- Be devoted to one another (Romans 12:10; 1 John 3:16).

- Be kind to one another (Ephesians 4:32).

- Be patient with one another (Ephesians 4:2; Colossians 3:13).

- Carry one another's burdens (Galatians 6:2).

- Comfort one another (1 Thessalonians 4:18; 5:11).

- Confess to one another (James 5:16).

- Encourage one another (Romans 14:19).

- Forgive one another (Ephesians 4:32; Colossians 3:13).

- Greet one another (Romans 16:16).

- Live in harmony with one another (Romans 12:16).

- Love one another (John 13:34; Romans 12:10; 1 Peter 1:22).

- Serve one another (Galatians 5:13; Philippians 2:3).

- Sing to one another (Ephesians 5:19).

- Spur one another on toward love and good deeds (Hebrews 10:24).

- Strengthen one another (Romans 14:19).

- Submit to one another (Ephesians 5:21; 1 Peter 5:5).

This list is also an excellent tool for evaluating aspects of our own or another person's maturity. We'll show how to use it later in this chapter.

"Hey, how's it going?" I (Marty) looked up from the speeches I was grading and found Brian standing in the doorway of my office. I welcomed him in and offered the chair next to my desk. He sat on the edge, as if he were ready to run if the conversation didn't go the way he hoped. Since I didn't know Brian, we chatted for a few moments about classes and college events. Finally, he mentioned that he'd come to see me about a specific request.

"My dad died when I was seven," he stammered. "I know this must sound strange, but I'm kind of looking for a dad figure in my life … I can't keep trying to make these kinds of decisions on my own."

"What decisions?" I asked.

"I'm interested in a girl here at the college, and since my last few attempts have been disasters, I thought you might be able to give me some advice."

Brian and I decided to meet weekly to pray and talk about relationships, God's will, and life in general. I never became a "dad" to Brian, but I did end up performing his wedding two years later. Brian made a good decision in choosing a wife, because he had reached the point in his maturity where he'd learned that neither dependence nor independence were the better parts of wisdom. He learned the value of interdependence—a quality that will carry him far in his marriage.

In an effort to help his students mature in this area, one of my (Marty's) colleagues and friends, Dr. Greg Trull, has each of his ministry majors sign a "Declaration of Interdependence." It reminds the students that neither dependence nor independence is the model for personal maturity. The declaration hangs for the entire year on his office door. Signing such a declaration may not guarantee relational growth, but it can serve as a constant reminder that maturity is marked by our ability to connect in a meaningful way with the people around us.

### Shifting from egocentricity to others-centricity

The immature believe that life is all about them. Their jobs, relationships, entertainment, and daily living arrangements are based on an underlying question, "What can I get out of this?" Emotional adolescents, they focus on their own feelings. For instance, it's not unusual for a newly married man to have conflicts with his wife over issues like what movies to watch, what cars to drive, and where to spend their vacation. While the mature husband finds great pleasure in making his wife happy, the immature husband rarely understands the life-changing benefits of sacrificing his personal time and pleasure.

*"Maturity begins to grow when you can sense your concern for others outweighing your concern for yourself."*
—John MacNaughton

A shift in this area aligns the relational gears, producing the potential for more meaningful relationships. As mature individuals begin to notice the needs of those around them, they begin to take responsibility for making each relationship successful and mutually pleasing. When this happens, the mature also become proactive.

### Shifting from passivity to proactivity

Immature people expect to be waited on. Many immature men live passively with wives who are passively waiting for them to figure out how their passivity is ruining the relationship. (That's a lot of passivity!) The mature are proactive.

*"Maturity is:*
*the ability to stick with a job until it's finished;*
*the ability to do a job without being supervised;*
*the ability to carry money without spending it;*
*and the ability to bear an injustice without wanting to get even."*
—Abigail Van Buren

Proactivity could be defined as doing the thing that needs doing before it looks like it needs to be done. The immature rarely keep a responsible job because they lack this characteristic.

More than one wife has shared with us how living with a passive man makes her feel less treasured, taken for granted. Many of the women would like their husbands to be spiritual leaders at home and at church. Men feel the same way about wives whose only interests are closets and clothes. Men would like their wives to share their hunger for God and the joy that comes from being in his presence. They want their wives to be proactive in lovemaking and, especially, in listening to the words that men aren't so sure they want to say. But, immature men and women lack the ability to be proactive because their lack of self-mastery makes them passive. When people become mature, they become proactive in nearly every area of their lives.

### Shifting from pleasure to purpose

The comfort zone is a shrine for adolescents. They refuse to recognize that growth and maturity are the results of tension and discomfort. A shift from pleasure-centeredness to purpose-centeredness occurs when the maturing person learns to push through discomfort and pain.

Who needs to suffer when we have patches for everything? Our laptop gets a virus and the manufacturer sends a software patch. Our back aches after a softball game and we stick on a pain patch—our lives are virtually pain free. This aversion to suffering prevents us from growing because growth rarely occurs in the comfort zone. God's patch for maturity sometimes includes pain.

To expect instant maturity without any discomfort is like an athlete expecting to be good at his sport without some pain—a kind of conflict between the brain and the body. Immaturity pleads with us "pain always hurts." Maturity replies, "Sometimes it helps."

### The shift from acquiring to applying

The last shift we observe in the transition from immaturity to maturity is a movement from the acquisition of knowledge to its application. It's not what a person knows that counts. The key to success is the effective application of our knowledge. When I (Rich) came out of college, I knew the techniques and theory of nearly every clinical test used in a hospital laboratory. The first day in the lab as an intern, I discovered the Complete Blood Count that took me three hours to do in college was routinely performed in several minutes by the medical technologist. My theoretical knowledge moved rapidly through practice to applied knowledge as I matured as a technologist. The immature can tell you what needs to be done, but only the mature do it.

Immaturity costs us considerable emotional energy. We lose friends, jobs, and what could be meaningful relationships. In every facet of our lives, immaturity causes conflicts which foster ill will and hard feelings.

*"You can only be young once. But you can always be immature."*
—Dave Barry

When maturity is missing in the home, observers are at a loss to tell who the children are—the parents or the kids. The parents many times have reversed the order of the childhood game, "show and tell." They *tell* the kids what to do, but have never *shown* them how. After decades of ministering to families, we find ourselves agreeing with others who maintain that immaturity may be the biggest problem our families face. Dennis Rainey, the Director of FamilyLife Ministries, stated in a recent conference that most of the men in the Evangelical church have not moved from adolescence to maturity. If he is right, immaturity is one of the leading causes of relational conflict. Before we can apply the steps for resolving conflicts caused by immaturity, we need to examine the interesting comparison with nature that God uses to explain growth.

## HUMAN GROWTH FERTILIZERS

In Psalms, the Bible's book of songs, God chose to describe a mature person as "a tree planted by streams of water"

(Psalm 1:3). Like many plants, if we're not raised with the right nutrients (love, discipline, etc.) we can still look alive—like a tree does during a dormant stage—while we're dying on the inside. God, the Grand Gardener, has a much more meaningful life waiting for us, but we'll miss its sweet fruit if we choose to skip the crucial nutrients. Examples in Scripture show that God uses at least four fertilizers to promote growth in our lives (all natural of course).

## Human Growth Fertilizers

1. People
2. Circumstances
3. The Church
4. The Bible

### Not so ordinary people

God specializes in using people who are further down the path of life than we are, who can be trusted with our deepest thoughts, who evidence a relational knowledge of God and a functional knowledge of the Bible, and who are willing to tell us the truth.

> *"The rate at which a person can mature is directly proportional to the embarrassment he can tolerate."*
> —Douglas Englebart

They are in the category we call "gardeners." They are not "sales reps." In a relationship, a sales rep. is someone who "aims to please." Many of us prefer to be sales reps. because we want our coworkers, family, and friends to appreciate our efforts. But, being a sales rep. is non-productive when someone needs to hear the truth. This is the role of the "gardener." The gardener is driven by the question Jesus

Christ asked the cripple alongside a well in Jerusalem, "Do you want to be healed?"

### Circumstances

"Gardener" friends help us to interpret our circumstances. For example, James wrote to the first-century Jewish Christians who were suffering rejection and persecution:

> Consider it pure joy, my brothers, whenever you face trials of many kinds, because you know that the testing of your faith develops perseverance. Perseverance must finish its work so that you may be mature and complete, not lacking anything (James 1:2–4).

When the recipients opened the letter, they were probably looking for a sales rep.'s advice. Instead they read, "Consider it pure joy ... whenever you face trials." Why would James say this? He knew that God uses not only people to promote growth, he also uses circumstances!

In the New Testament book of Hebrews, we are reminded that since we are sons and daughters, God is in the business of disciplining us.

> If you are not disciplined (and everyone undergoes discipline), then you are illegitimate children and not true sons. Moreover, we have all had human fathers who disciplined us and we respected them for it. How much more should we submit to the Father of our spirits and live! ... God disciplines us for our good, that we may share in his holiness. No discipline seems pleasant at the time, but painful. Later on, however, it produces a harvest of righteousness and peace for those who have been trained by it (Hebrews 12:7–11).

It is unfortunate that our culture has limited the meaning of "discipline" to "punishment." The Greek word for discipline, *paideia,* is primarily used of "rearing and guiding a child toward maturity."[3] It describes the involved kind of dad who puts his son on a bicycle, cheers, and holds the seat as the boy wobbles down the road.

> *"Viewing the child solely as an immature person*
> *is a way of escaping comforting him."*
> —Clark Moustakas

### The Church

There are a growing number of Christians who believe the local church is unnecessary. Although it is not the purpose of this book to argue this, it is important to note that the Apostle Paul, in his letter to the church in Ephesus, said that gifts were given to the church to equip God's people for ministry and maturity (Ephesians 4:12–14).

> *"Full maturity is achieved by realizing*
> *that you have choices to make."*
> —Angela Barron McBride

Like many of us, John wanted the loneliness and pain to end. He was willing to do almost anything to get Cherie back. After several weeks of Bible studies and meetings with the pastor, John realized that he needed to grow up for himself (not to get Cherie back). The church provided the ongoing encouragement and accountability John needed.

### The Bible

John began to experience the nurturing of the Holy Spirit through the rich fertilizing factors of practical Bible study. Like the psalm writer, John discovered that the Bible provided "a lamp" so that he could see where his feet were currently positioned on the road to maturity and "a light" for understanding the path ahead (119:105). Over the next year, John learned to control his temper and complain less. He became more thankful and more interested in his wife's hobbies. As of this printing, they are still not back under the same roof, but they've started sitting together at church and she is smiling again. The turnover rate at work has slowed, because John now believes he has a purpose God wants him to fulfill in each of his employee's lives. (They're no longer simply there for his profit and pleasure.) John has a long way to go, but not as far as when he first started.

## RULES FOR ENCOURAGING MATURITY

John's wife Cherie is also in counseling at the church. She's currently learning the following rules so that she can help John if they do get back together.

*"I would say that the surest measure of a man's or woman's maturity is the harmony, style, joy, and dignity he creates in his marriage, and the pleasure and inspiration he provides for his spouse."*
—Benjamin Spock

### Rule 1: Own your behavior

We love the blame game. Whenever we're cornered by a caring friend, we find it easier to blame than to own our behavior. In a culture where victim status helps maintain the economy it's even easier to play and win. However, when we act out of this kind of immaturity, we don't resolve the issue. We lose track of the reason for the quarrel and the conflict remains. The first rule in resolving this kind of conflict is to control our own behavior. Although John is working on this in specific areas such as yelling and complaining, Cherie is working on it, too, because the same rule applies when we confront someone's immaturity.

Whenever we are preparing to confront someone, we need to determine how we are going to respond to their use of tactics like the blame game. We need to think through our likely responses and compare those behaviors to the Bible's teachings about graceful speech (see Colossians 4:6).

One of the wisest ways to begin this kind of conversation is to say something like:

"I'm not here to pretend that my life is perfect or that I'm already mature, but I do want you to understand that a specific behavior is causing conflict in our relationship. I want you to own that behavior and, especially, to begin working on it. I forgive you and I'm looking forward to what our relationship will become in the future."

Owning our behaviors provides the right atmosphere for the immature to own theirs.

### Rule 2: Wait for the right time

Again, we must stress the importance of timing. The best time is not when a person is acting out his or her immature behavior. If we are willing to wait until the right time, we may discover more effective solutions. There are times when the immature are ready to consider the issue from a more calm and mature perspective. If we "jump the gun" we may have the right words, but they will be lost in the wrong moment.

### Rule 3: Get others involved

John Wooden lived by the maxim, "Make friends before you need them." The worst time to start making friends is *when* you need them. When we are in crisis, we look like the black hole of despair and no one wants to be involved with us. Your closest friends can help you redeem the relationship, so get them involved.

> *"Make friends before you need them."*
> —John Wooden

### Rule 4: Attack the root

It's a mistake to discuss the slamming of doors rather than the immaturity that led to such action. We often react to the symptom of immaturity rather than the cause. It would have been a mistake to address John's temper without addressing his immaturity. Some anger management classes would have taught him how to manage rather than replace his temper.

## Rule 5: Record and reward

When I (Rich) served as a Dean of Students, I'd meet with the resident hall staff each month. Our specific agenda at the meeting in November was to see if any students needed to be asked to leave. Each time we discussed a student, I'd read from an anecdotal calendar I kept. Often the anecdotes would show that the particular student had five behavioral incidents in September, two in October, and only one in November. The calendar demonstrated his or her growth. Of course, you may also discover that behaviors remain unchanged (or are escalating). In that case, it may be necessary to implement the next rule.

### Changing the Frequency: Conflicts Caused by Immaturity

You can use the following to reduce the frequency of conflicts caused by immaturity.

1. List evidences of immaturity (phrases, body language, and actions) on your calendar (or PDA). (You can use abbreviations such as SF for "sassy face.")

2. If the evidence of immaturity appears again, write the abbreviation on the day it occurred.

3. At the end of the week, reward any decrease in frequency. This will encourage you as well as the individual who is struggling with immaturity.

4. If the behavior isn't changing in frequency, respectfully and gently share the evidence in your calendar with the individual. Then use Rules 6 and 7.

## Rule 6: Raise the stakes

Cherie raised the stakes when she left the note for John. After leaving the note, she called a counselor at our church and explained what she had done.

"What would it take for you to take him back?" The counselor asked. The question pushed Cherie to put together a plan which became like a contract between her and her husband. The counselor warned her that when John called and was filled with remorse, Cherie's first urge would be to let him resume his role in the home. Experience had convinced the counselor that if Cherie did this, John would never mature.

## Rule 7: Remember how God answers

Sometimes when we pray, God begins to change the situation by making it worse. Most of the Jewish leaders in the New Testament prayed that the Messiah would come and end religious persecution by setting up a heavenly kingdom on earth, but God initially answered these prayers by sending an even more persecuted Jesus to set up a heavenly kingdom in their hearts. Sometimes, when dealing with immaturity, God answers our prayers by making a situation, temporarily, worse.

Whether we are immature or suffer the consequences of being around immature people, there is a way out: we can redeem relationships damaged by immaturity.

**Steps to Redeeming Relationships Damaged by Immaturity**

Step 1:     Own your behavior

Step 2:     Wait for the right time

Step 3:     Get others involved

Step 4:     Attack the root

Step 5:     Record and reward

Step 6:     Raise the stakes

Step 7:     Remember how God answers

**BOLD IDEAS**

Immaturity is different from the other causes for conflict. It influences how we see the world around us.

Humans have been given a pause button which can be pushed to suspend a response to stimuli.

The comfort zone is a shrine for adolescents.

Immaturity pleads with us, "pain always hurts." Maturity replies, "Sometimes it helps."

Owning our behaviors provides the right atmosphere for the immature to own theirs.

If we "jump the gun" we may have the right words, but they will be lost in the wrong moment.

Sometimes when we pray, God begins to change the situation by making it worse.

CHAPTER SEVEN

SOLUTION

# Belief or Opinion?
# The Black, the White, and the Gray

*There are as many opinions as there are people:*
*each has his own correct way.*
—Terence, 190–159 B.C.

*Jesus said, "Go and make disciples," not converts to your opinions.*
—Oswald Chambers

Several years ago, I (Rich) was asked to pastor a church in the Northwest that had lost its senior pastor and much of the congregation shortly after replacing the piano with drums, guitars, and a keyboard. To determine if these changes had caused the exodus, one of the associate pastors and I agreed to visit families that had left in the past few months.

As we sat in the Franklins' living room, I explained that if they had left the church because something had offended them, we wanted to right that wrong. I could taste the tension. Finally, Beth Franklin cleared her throat,

"Pastor, you're just too liberal for us."

I was stunned! I looked at her calmly, but my mind was screaming, *Liberal? Most liberals would deny me membership to their club!* Still, with manufactured calm I asked, "What makes you think I'm liberal?"

"Your music is worldly and the way the lights are dimmed during the prayer time seems artificial." I wanted to quote Andy Rooney who once joked, "A great many people do not have a right to their own opinions because they don't know what they are talking about," but I refrained. I was still torqued in my mind when I saw the tears in her eyes. I realized that she honestly believed we were a liberal church. The other pastor and I left with aching hearts because this situation reminded us, again, that differing beliefs—how we determine what's black, white, and gray—cause most of the relational conflict in the church.

## ABSOLUTE LIBERTY?

If you have grown up in conservative churches as we have, you've probably experienced the divisiveness caused when we confuse areas of "absolutes" (for example, what the Bible teaches about God's character) with areas of liberty (for example, the style of music we use to worship him). As one writer stated,

> You would think that Christian liberty would be a very pleasant doctrine, but to teach it threatens our stranglehold on "truth" as we define it. I'm not talking about the core essentials of salvation, but all the other peripheral issues that have divided Christians into almost 3000 different "flavors." We don't hear much about Christian liberty because we're afraid people might actually take hold of it and not do things OUR way.[1]

At the church where I (Rich) am a pastor, we have experienced the frustration of losing good people over "flavors." People leave the church over issues related to polity, percussion or pianos, but if you asked them, they say they it was because of "doctrine." The irony is that our church's doctrinal statement hasn't changed in its thirty-five years of existence!

## FLAVOR FIGHTS

Conflicts happen whenever we make our preferences or "flavors" part of God's requirements (or more important than someone else's preferences). I (Marty) learned in a junior high Sunday school class that our church didn't use electric guitars because "Satan can enter a church service through the electricity." Imagine my dilemma that night when I reached over to turn on the lamp next to my bed! That week at prayer meeting my youth pastor chuckled when I asked for clarification. "Obviously, Satan doesn't need electricity to enter a service," he said.

Charles Elliott Newbold, Jr. explains the seriousness such conflict creates:

> Two Churches of Christ exist in a small Tennessee town where, according to their own doctrine, only one should have existed. One group believed it was okay to have a kitchen in their church building and the other did not. So they split.[2]

Whenever we confuse biblical absolutes with opinions, we create conflict and we bypass primary scriptural commands in order to focus on secondary commands.

For example, holiness and purity are crucial aspects of our character, but they are secondary goals. Our primary goal is to love God with all of our hearts and love each other with this God-given love. This is what Jesus Christ clearly said summarized the whole Old Testament writings. When we love God and others, purity and holiness *will* characterize our lives. Unfortunately, when we bypass *love* to reach holiness and purity, we become meanspirited. Our attitudes, our body language, and our tone of voice create conflict. Even if our opinion wins the day, we end up trading unity for uniformity (and they're not the same). Like a cryptic code, the diagram below can help us redeem relationships riddled by this kind of conflict. Those who are "good" at relationships (warm and wonderful to be around) have deciphered the code and learned the wisdom that enables them to reduce, and sometimes avoid, this kind of relational conflict. The code involves three ways we should think about *our* beliefs and opinions or the beliefs and opinions of *others*.

| Black | Gray | White |
|-------|------|-------|

The column labeled "Black" represents the things the Bible instructs us to avoid. These are the "Thou shalt nots" of the Christian life. The second column labeled "Gray" represents the things that are not specifically addressed by Scripture. Our guideline for these things is wisdom. Here, the Bible gives us principles to guide our decisions. The third column labeled "white" includes everything the believer is commanded to do.

*One of the misconceptions of the black, the white, and the gray is that the lines between them change with the culture.*

A line separates the black from the gray. This line is drawn, not in the sands of opinion, but in Scripture. It never moves. God will never accept sexual sin or stealing. He will never condone pride and arrogance. He will never desire that his children be less than loving and holy in their character. God's "black" and "white" items parallel his character and are unchangeable.

| Black | Gray | White |
|---|---|---|
| The Christian is commanded not to do these things. | The Christian must decide whether or not he or she will be involved in these. | The Christian is commanded to do these things. |
| *Obedience is expected* | *Wisdom is needed* | *Obedience is expected* |

The believer is commanded to obey the absolutes of God's Word (the black and white). The activities and behaviors seen in the "gray" area include activities that may be neither right nor wrong. These require wisdom. For matters in the black or white, ask, "What does God's Word command me to do in this area?" For matters in the gray, ask, "What is the wisest thing for me to do?"

## Understanding the "black"

The black area is characterized by six factors. When these factors are understood, we are able to understand why living life from the perspective of prohibition (the black) is unfulfilling. A large number of us live in the "black." We like following lists of rules because they provide an easy way of measuring our success. If I struggle with stealing, I know that if I eliminate it from my life, I will have achieved something significant (notice the number of I's in the sentence). One of the problems with this approach (besides the pride) is that I become preoccupied with abstaining. Ironically, I end up measuring my life by counting the things I subtract.

**Discerning the difference between black, white, and gray areas**

| Black | Gray | White |
|---|---|---|
| 1. Measurable success | 1. Difficult to measure | 1. Difficult to measure |
| 2. Focused on abstinence | 2. Focused on wisdom and deference | 2. Focused on obedience |
| 3. Grades sin | 3. Validates actions | 3. Grades virtue |
| 4. Absolutes based | 4. Principles based | 4. Motives based |
| 5. Associated with a critical spirit | 5. Associated with extreme attitudes | 5. Associated with accommo- dation |
| 6. Makes no provision for the "gray" | 6. Weighs the "black" and the "white" | 6. Fulfills the law |

### *Focused on abstinence*

One of the greatest impediments of the church's outreach is our approach that says, "God's gift is a list of things that will make you feel good when you stop doing them." To borrow a MacArthurism, "nothing could be further from the truth." When we operate in the "black" we forget that God's gift to us is mostly "addition" with some "subtraction" thrown in. We are feasting on the fruit of the Spirit, not just fasting from Satan's garbage. Although giving things up will result *from* the gift of salvation, abstinence is not the gift.

*The un-churched perceive Christianity as a religion*
*whose price for joining is abstaining.*

Jesus Christ's contemporaries struggled with this, too. The religious leaders of his day had made the Law a heavy "black and white" burden. While the religious stacked more rules in the oxcart of Jewish requirements, Jesus offered to pull the yoke and provide rest (Matthew 11:28). He wasn't preoccupied with the black. Jesus seemed to break most of the gray rules, yet Scripture teaches that he completely fulfilled the Law's true intent.

### Grading sin

Living in the "black" feels like wearing an old pair of leather shoes. The list we create forms comfortably around our feet and helps us walk the straight and narrow. However, eventually the leather of our mind softens as we begin to place different values on the prohibited items mentioned in the Bible. We grade sin on a scale of 1 to 10—with God only reluctantly forgiving #10 sins. For example, sexual sin is always a #10 sin. Pride, on the other hand, is often treated as a #1 or #2 sin.

### A critical spirit

*"Whenever you are in a critical temper,*
*it is impossible to enter into communion with God."*
—Oswald Chambers

Those who walk in these shoes believe that being right about a behavior gives them the responsibility to share their belief—whether it agrees with Scripture or not. This kind of sharing doesn't have to create conflict, but it does when it contradicts love's patience, kindness, gentleness (1 Corinthians 13) and respect (1 Peter 3:15).

*"Criticism is the disapproval of people not for having faults*
*but for having faults different from our own."*

—Anonymous

### Away with the "gray"

Early in the twentieth century, a few seminaries began to deny the veracity and authenticity of the Bible. Carl McIntyre and J. Gresham Machen helped lead a counter movement that separated from these schools. Both had been educated at Princeton and were appalled as the seminary embraced this new approach to the Bible. As a result, Carl McIntyre helped form the Bible Presbyterian Church, while Machen helped start the Orthodox Presbyterian Church. Why two different churches? McIntyre began condemning cultural practices in America, while Machen maintained that most of those practices were not condemned in Scripture. The result? Separate churches. Timothy George uses this example to show how confusing biblical absolutes (black and white areas) with matters of liberty (gray areas) can damage relationships:

> There were two reasons for this schism. One was McIntyre's insistence on total abstinence from alcohol, an issue the Machen group considered a matter of Christian liberty, while the Holiness and pietist traditions had long emphasized the importance of a Christian life separated from the world—no alcohol, tobacco, dancing, cards, or theater, along with no short skirts or bobbed hair for women.[3]

McIntyre made little allowance for the "gray." His recipe for righteousness lumped alcohol, tobacco, dancing, cards, theater, dress, and bobbed hair into the same bowl as denying Scripture. He overstirred the issues and the result was relational conflict between men who had originally fought side by side.

The church today finds itself in the same battle with the culture. So, Phillip Yancey warns us, "In a thoroughly secular culture, the church is more likely to show ungrace through a spirit of moral superiority or a fierce attitude toward opponents in the 'culture wars.'"[4] Moral superiority and fierce attitudes develop when we try to dye the "gray" areas in our culture "black" or "white."

## Understanding the "white"

As the chart indicates, the "white" column is characterized by six similar factors.

Looking at some of the *differences* between the black and white columns (this time in reverse order) will help us reduce the frequency of these kinds of conflicts.

### Fulfills the law

The Apostle Paul stuns us with a remarkable statement: "Loving people fulfills the law!" That's like saying to people who live in the "black" column, "every sin on your list is avoided when you truly love other people." In fact, that's essentially what Paul said.

> Let no debt remain outstanding, except the continuing debt to love one another, for he who loves his fellow man has fulfilled the law. [9] The commandments, "Do not commit adultery," "Do not murder," "Do not steal," "Do not covet," and whatever other commandment there may be, are summed up in this one rule: "Love your neighbor as yourself." [10] Love does no harm to its neighbor. Therefore love is the fulfillment of the law (Romans 13:8–10).

### Motives based

Some believe that when the Apostle Paul says "let no debt remain outstanding," he is simply talking about not owing anyone anything. They use it as a proof text to show that we should not be in financial debt. But Paul is saying so much more: We may be current in paying our bills, but we will never be "paid-up" in loving others. Paul reminds the church in Galatia that the only thing that counts in the final analysis is faith being worked out in love (Galatians 5:6). And, he reminds the church in Corinth that everything we do without love is just noise and lip sync (1 Corinthians 13:1–4).

> *Rather than living a life of prohibition,*
> *we need to live a life of love.*

It's not good enough that I refuse to steal a person's wife or possessions. This only demonstrates that I am not an adulterer or a thief. However, if I love my neighbor I will not steal his wife or goods because I love him (and her). When I become a loving person, I not only accomplish the law, but I do it with the right motive.

### Difficult to measure

While most of the items listed in the "black" are measurable (stealing and lying are examples), most items listed in the "white" are not. What does love look like? What does holiness look like? When I am commanded to forgive, what actual steps do I take? While the spiritually immature live according to a list of measurable absolutes, it takes maturity to measure abstracts. Loving others and applying the exhortations of the "white" to our lives, helps us avoid everything in the "black."

### Associated with accommodation

When I (Marty) lived by lists, I was critical of every behavior that didn't meet my measurement of right and wrong. I wanted to make sure everyone had the same list I did. The minute I began *loving* others, I became easier to be around. My reputation became associated with a gentler, more respectful way of life.

## Understanding the "gray"

The "gray" column includes the same six factors. The major difference concerns the fourth aspect: The "gray" is based in principles, not prohibitions.

### *Principles, not prohibitions*

Years ago I (Rich) had a Christian neighbor who believed that you could not mow your lawn on Sundays. To him, it was sacrilege. I believed that it was OK to mow. Who was right? It's a logical question that often leads to illogical answers. The truth is what may be good for you may never be good for me. Since the Holy Spirit often uses the "gray" to develop our *individual* relationship with God and our ministries, we need to be careful not to create conflict where he is creating character.

---

**Changing the Frequency: Conflicts Caused by Opinions**

Paul's counsel in Romans 14 can help us reduce the frequency of these conflicts:

1. Be strong for the weak (verse 1),

2. Don't be the judge (verses 3 and 22),

3. Don't be a problem (verses 15 and 21),

4. Don't offend your conscience (verses 14 and 22),

5. Be an example (verses 16–18) and a peace promoter (verse 19).

The Apostle Paul faced the same kinds of conflict as people from different cultural backgrounds formed the first churches. Appropriately, the principles he lists in Chapter 14 of his letter to the church in Rome can help us with these conflicts.

A friend, Talya, remembers her senior prom. Earlier that week one of her Christian friends asked if she would double-date with her. Talya was stunned. She thought Christians didn't go to dances.

When she asked her dad, he slammed his coffee mug on the table, "You know the answer!"

"Why?" Talya asked

"Are you challenging my authority? No, should be enough!" He growled.

Talya would be shocked to learn the truth: Her dad didn't know the answer. He had no Bible verses for his prohibition on dancing. He retreated behind parental authority to win the conflict. A dad guided by the motive of love would have resolved the matter differently, even if he had strong convictions about dancing. Wise parents emphasize the exhortations of Scripture (Romans 13:8) over the prohibitions. They understand that love leads to obedience, but that obedience does not always lead to love.

## REPAIRING RELATIONSHIPS

We have used the following outline to help people repair relationships damaged by beliefs and opinions. Think about it the way you think about maintaining your car. It's like a 6-point inspection (but we'll warn you—it costs a lot more than money).

### Check your lines

Most of us have very little "gray" in our personal lives. As we look at aspects of our culture, we adjust the lines for the "black," the "white" and the "gray." The gray is small for me (Rich) since I have decided whether or not I will do most of the things found there. They are still in the gray, but I have moved the lines so that they fit into either the black or white for me personally. I don't hold others to the same standard. They're my convictions.

Sometimes, we move the line so things that really belong in the gray become part of the black list. They have been forbidden to us for so long we have forgotten how they got there. Other times we move the lines so that things end up in the white (as commandments) when they should be considered matters of wisdom.

The deciding factor is not how we "feel" about these issues, but what Scripture (the repair manual) actually teaches. (Disney's recurring movie theme of "trust your heart" doesn't help us here.)

When I (Marty) started working in Christian ministry, I was convinced that drinking wine was a sin. I was appalled to discover that some Christian traditions actually use *real wine* during their time of communion (remembering Christ's death and resurrection by eating a small piece of bread and drinking a small amount of juice or wine). When I studied the passages in the Bible, I quickly realized that I was wrong. When I read that the Apostle Paul instructed a young pastor, Timothy, to drink a little wine for his stomach aches and that Paul used the same word when he said not to get drunk with wine but to be filled with the Spirit, I realized that the word couldn't logically refer to "grape juice" as I had been taught. Although I didn't want to change my view since I had seen the devastation of alcoholism, I knew I had to. I still don't drink today (because alcoholism runs in my family), but I've eliminated all relational conflict in this area. In fact, many of the members of the church I pastored in Italy have wine every evening. The Scriptures adjusted the line, so I adjusted my life.

## Check your attitude

Most conflict in these areas is accompanied by attitude! It is amazing how judgmental or condescending we can be. Years ago, after performing a wedding for a great Christian couple, I (Rich) became irritated when I realized that they were going to have dancing at their reception. They even had a DJ! Our relationship was ruined. "How could they do this to my reputation as a pastor?" I pouted. Again, I felt the Holy Spirit reminding me that this is an issue belonging in the gray. So I checked my attitude. I let the "gray" move me to grace. No one (except for my wife) was aware I was bothered. The relationship was redeemed before the couple even knew it had been damaged.

### Check your motive

Are we trying to impress others? Maybe we believe right behavior wins kudos with the Lord. Some of us might actually believe that although we are saved by placing faith in Jesus Christ, we maintain our salvation by doing the right things.

Actually the only time we do right in God's eyes is when our motives are love and faith. Other motives blur the distinctions and soon the "black," the "white" and the "gray" lines move far away from the priorities of loving God and our neighbors. When we check our motives, most ruined relationships can be reestablished.

### Check your service record

You can always know whether you are a servant by the way you respond when treated as one. Only a servant can apply the principles that we have listed. Years ago I (Rich) memorized something I heard John Powell say: "We need to learn to use things and love people rather than love things and use people." Powell reminds us that we need love rather than use.

When I (Marty) talk in the men's dorms at the college, the men often request a message called, "The Toilet Test of Truth." It's a lesson that compares cleaning toilets to Jesus's first century command to wash each other's feet (John

13:14). The conclusion usually causes a ruckus because I use overstatement to make this point: "If you don't regularly clean toilets here in this dorm, you haven't learned to be a servant." The usual objections include things like "Our dorm fees pay for that" or "That could be dangerous" (obviously someone who's never cleaned one). But I don't relent. "It's the toilet test of truth," I remind them. "Our character is tested by how we handle the ugly tasks." The same goes for conflict resolution. Most of our conflicts in this area are solved (or decrease in intensity) when we serve other people's opinions and beliefs instead of favoring our own.

### Check your convictions

Some years ago, I (Rich) believed that Christian rock music was wrong. My then teenage daughter, Jennifer, asked me to drive her around town one Saturday. She shared her plan to spend the afternoon playing Christian rock to me. She wanted me to hear the music and tell her why it was the wrong kind to listen to. She was willing to give it up, but she wanted to understand why.

As we drove around listening to her music, I began to hear the words. They were words that spoke spiritual truth to the changing life of a teenager. They were speaking truth to me. That afternoon, I changed my position. Rather than trying to convince, I was willing to be convinced.

### Check your conscience

*Caution: Don't reduce your life to the weakest conscience.*

We are not suggesting that we let everyone determine how we live our lives. There are two groups of people in the church. One group is moldable and truly sensitive. There are many times when new Christians are on a search for the next step in their spiritual journey. Only when we defer to them will we earn the right to become a mentor and help them to the next step.

The second group is looking for a fight. They want everyone to play by their rules. If you allow this group to create the rules, they will suck the life out of you. We have a guideline at our (Rich's) church: "We will not reduce our ministry to the weakest conscience." It works for interpersonal relationships, too.

The Pharisees had a weak conscience. They did not appreciate the ministry of Jesus Christ in their lives. Jesus aimed his words at them when he warned, "Do not give dogs what is sacred; do not throw your pearls to pigs. If you do, they may trample them under their feet, and then turn and tear you to pieces" (Matthew 7:6). Jesus cautions us to be careful when we communicate the things of God (pearls) to unholy people (pigs) because they will not appreciate what is being done for them.

## REDEEMED RELATIONSHIPS

Some of the most painful conflicts in our lives can come from our opinions and personal beliefs. We began this chapter with our experience in the Franklin home. That night was not the end of the story.

> "Your music is worldly, and the way the lights are dimmed during the prayer time seems artificial . . . ."

The next day another couple, the Johnsons, came by the church office to talk. I (Rich) assumed we were going to have a repeat of the Franklins. Jim Johnson started the conversation before I could.

"Dr. Rollins, we came to tell you that we have decided to return to the church." I smiled as Jim continued, "We grew up in homes where we were taught that anyone who used any Bible other than the King James Version was a liberal. We believe that we've been wrong. We're uncomfortable with the changes at the church, but we trust the leadership. To be honest, for the first time in our lives, we come to church excited about experiencing God's presence."

God wants all of us to be willing to challenge our preconceived ideas about how to live the Christian life. When we find freedom and clarity in the areas of the black, the white, and the gray, we discover the wisdom necessary for redeeming our relationships.

BOLD IDEAS

How we determine what's black, white and gray causes most of the relational conflict in the church.

We create conflict when we confuse what is important with what is not.

When we bypass love to reach holiness and purity, we can easily become meanspirited.

We grade sin on a scale of 1 to 10—with God only reluctantly forgiving #10 sins.

The church today finds itself at war with the culture.

Loving people fulfills the law.

Rather than living a life of prohibition, we need to live a life of love.

Some of us actually believe that although we are saved by placing faith in Jesus Christ, we maintain our salvation by doing the right things.

You can always know whether you are a servant by the way you respond when treated like one.

## CHAPTER EIGHT

SOLUTION

# MENDING MARRIAGE:
# ONE + ONE = ONE?

*Getting married is easy. Staying married is more difficult.
Staying happily married for a lifetime
should rank among the fine arts.*
—Roberta Flack

One plus one never equaled one in our math classrooms,
so why do we think it will in our living rooms? The "two
shall become one" Bible passage from Ephesians 5 sounds
romantic at the wedding, but when the tests come, it feels
like a 50-page story problem waiting to flunk us from our
first semester of calculus. Why is it so hard to learn the new
math?

The sooner we realize that marriage is a *cause* of conflict
(not just a part of it) the sooner we'll be able to do the
addition. Think about the last "discussion" you had with
your spouse. Sure, it might have been caused by expectations
or crushed character, but it might have just been that the
two of you are in the most poignant of all *relationships*. (The
*relation* part of the word means the two of you. The *ship* part

means you can experience a wreck at any moment!) As you "discussed," you pointed out options, arranged supporting materials and finally decided the potential wreck wasn't worth all the effort (after all, there was a slight possibility *you* could be wrong). That's probably why humorist Don Fraser could write "A happy home is one in which each spouse grants the possibility that the other may be right, though neither believes it."

So far we've discussed several causes of conflict. Although, separately, these can create havoc, in marriage we experience all of them together! When we consider all of these opposing forces pitted against the modern marriage, it is a miracle that any marriage works.

*"Statistics reveal that many marriages either dissolve*
*or are robbed of intimacy and satisfaction*
*because of the couple's inability to effectively resolve conflict."*
—Dr. Todd E. Linaman

## TOGETHER, ALL ALONE

The first chapters of the Bible describe the spectacular creative act of God as he speaks the world and the universe into existence. After making man, God acknowledges that it isn't good for man to be alone. God's solution is to make Adam a counterpart, "a helper suitable for him" (Genesis 2:16). Then God does a strange thing. Instead of saying, "Adam, do you realize that you have no helper?" and then presenting Eve, he gives Adam the chore of naming the animals.

> Now the Lord God had formed out of the ground all the beasts of the field and all the birds of the air. He brought them to the man to see what he would name them; and whatever the man called each living creature, that was its name. So the man gave names to all the livestock, the birds of the air and all the

beasts of the field. But for Adam no suitable helper was found
(Genesis 2:19–20).

Adam's naming of the animals was not designed simply
to give him a part in God's creative act. The concept of
naming referred to in this passage goes beyond calling
a bear a bear or a platypus a platypus. We believe he was
identifying their unique qualities. God's goal was not to have
Adam take credit for the first taxonomy but to bring him
to the realization that all of the animals had counterparts
except him. Adam, after naming the animals, came to the
conclusion that he was alone.

Then God created Eve from Adam's own genetic
material (his rib). The Hebrew poem implies that they
complemented each other and that, in Eve, Adam found
relief from the tension created by knowing he was alone.
We have no idea how much time elapses between Chapters
2 and 3. But we do know that the story takes a detour.

> *"Men and women are not from different planets.*
> *They're both from earth."*
>
> —Mark Goulston

In Chapter 3, the serpent comes to Eve to challenge her
dependence on God. Satan tempts her to strike out on her
own. "After all," he argues, "God knows when you eat of the
tree of the knowledge of good and evil that you will become
like him." It wasn't a lie. Afterward, in verse 22, God says
"The man has now become like one of us, knowing good
and evil." However, it asserts the saddest irony of the human
race: That in becoming like God we became separated from
him and each other.

After eating from the tree of the knowledge of good and
evil, Eve gives some fruit to Adam and he eats. While Eve
was deceived, Adam was not (1 Timothy 2:13). His choice
was difficult. He could have thought to himself, "Do I keep

God and lose my wife or do I keep my wife and lose God?"
He chose the latter and, because of his choice, sin sank its
fangs into the heart of humanity—mankind had fallen (1
Corinthians 15:22).

Later, after explaining the consequences of Adam's
action, God turns his attention to Eve. "To the woman he
[God] said, 'I will greatly increase your pains in childbearing;
with pain you will give birth to children. Your *desire* will be
for your husband, and he will *rule* over you'" (Genesis 3:16,
emphasis added).

This is one of the most misunderstood passages of
Scripture. The last sentence of verse 16 has traditionally
been interpreted this way: "You will have sexual desire for
your husband and he will be in charge of you." However, as
many Old Testament scholars have pointed out, the context
is concerned with more than "sexual desire." The same
Hebrew word translated "desire" occurs again in Genesis
Chapter 4.

> Then the Lord said to Cain, "Why are you angry? Why is your
> face downcast? If you do what is right, will you not be accepted?
> But if you do not do what is right, sin is crouching at your door;
> it *desires* to have you, but you must master it." (Genesis 4:6–7,
> emphasis ours)

Understanding this passage helps us understand one of
the sources of conflict in marriage. Clearly the word is used
in Chapter 4 to imply control. What, then, was God saying
to Eve in Chapter 3? Ron Allen suggests the following:

> I will bring something new into the wonder of the bringing of
> children into the world.

> I will greatly magnify your pain in giving birth. When you give
> birth to your children it will be in physical pain.

> I will also allow pain to come into your marriage relationship
> with your husband.

You will tend to desire to usurp the role I have given to him as the compassionate leader in your home, rejecting his role and belittling his manhood.

And the man on his part will tend to relate to you in loveless tyranny, dominating and stifling your integrity as an equal partner to himself.[1]

From that day on, conflict over who's in charge became a reality in the husband-wife relationship. Allen continues, "If this is an accurate reflection of the intention of this curse on the woman, it is a curse indeed that has lasted through time. No wonder there is such discord among married couples." It's this conflict that causes us to be able to live together, but still feel like we're all alone.

Any history student will remember the battle American women had to wage to gain the same freedoms enjoyed by their male counterparts. In 1878 the women's suffrage amendment was presented to Congress for enactment, but the members refused to vote on it—until World War I (1917), when the Suffragists asked, "How can America fight for freedom on foreign shores when half of America's population hasn't been granted liberty?" Two years later, on June 4, 1919, the United States Senate passed the amendment by one vote. Finally, women would have the same rights as men. Really?

Look at almost any field of pursuit in America where men have been prominent and you will find women still struggling for equality. The curse in Eden, which predicted that men and women would experience conflict with each other, extends into our modern culture.

*"Love, honor and negotiate."*
—Alan Loy McGinnis

## THE CONFLICT OF CONTROL

Like men, women contribute to marital conflict when they put their energies into trying to take control. Some try to establish control by threatening their husbands, others use emotion and tears, while others withhold sex. This was Patti's approach with Hal.

Patti met Hal at a singles event at church and they married a year later. Hal was a strong personality. He managed the money in the marriage. He held the household hostage and questioned Patti's expenditures item by item. Early in their marriage, Patti thought that having Hal grocery shop with her would be fun. After several shopping trips where Hal took things out of the cart because he didn't think they needed them, Patti started shopping when Hal was at work.

When Patti wanted something, she knew how to get it. Hal wanted sex several times a week and Patti knew it. Patti learned that if she withheld sex for a couple of nights, Hal would give her the money she wanted to buy those "unnecessary items" on her list. He complained about it, but she got her way. This manipulation, motivated by the desire to control, devastated their love for each other.

The Apostle Paul encourages Christian couples to relate to each other in a way that meets their needs and brings hope to their relationship. In Ephesians 5, Paul exhorts husbands to love their wives, indicating that marriage should reflect the love of Christ, not the rebellion of the fall in the Garden of Eden.

But Paul also gives us God's solution to the conflict introduced in the garden. "Each one of you also must love his wife as he loves himself, and the wife must respect her husband" (Ephesians 5:33). Because he created us, God knows that men need respect and women need love. Dr. Mark Goulston confirmed this fact when he wrote, "In my twenty-five years in private practice, one of the few things that has remained a constant is that most women want to be cherished and most men want to be admired."[2] Dr. Emerson E. Eggerichs agrees. In 1999, Dr. Eggerichs launched Love and Respect Conferences to communicate his belief that love and respect are universal qualities that are essential to a successful marriage.

Women need to be loved and tend to interpret their relationships based on that need. Men need to be respected and interpret their relationships based on that need. God, knowing we have those needs says, "Husbands, love your wives" and "Wives, respect your husbands." Respect and love can redeem relationships torn apart by the desire to control.

### Changing the Frequency: Getting "Out of Control"

1. When controlling people get in your face, forget getting in theirs. Get in their heart instead. Ask, "Why is having control in this specific instance so important to you?"

2. The answer to the question in item 1 will make it easier for you to submit. Submission will usually lead to remission. (The desire to control may not go away, but it will not continue to damage your relationship.)

### In one respect or another

When a wife is disrespectful in the way she treats her husband she deeply hurts the relationship. A woman who is married to a jerk is best served if she doesn't respond like one. Like him, in the middle of conflict, she must be truthful and respectful at the same time.

Once they're shown respect, most men will feel loved. Contrary to their natural tendency, wives *can* be empowered to stop trying to take control of their husbands. They *can* stop trying to remake him into something he is not. Of course, every wife sees potential in her husband that he may not see. *A godly wife brings out that potential in her husband by respecting him.* Respect is important because each of us was made in the image of God. When the husband is "acting like he's eighteen again," a wise wife knows when and how to remind him of his *real* age. She doesn't deliberately choose words to make him feel foolish. She doesn't "put him down." She shows respect in the language and gestures she chooses to express herself. She shows respect when she treats him according to what he could be rather than on the basis of who he is at the moment.

### Ready, Set, Respect: Respecting a Husband

**Words**

1. Stick a 3 x 5 card in his wallet or lunch box that says, "I haven't told you lately, but I respect ... ." (whatever you respect about him)

2. When he looks at you longingly, before your lips touch, whisper "You know what I respect about you?" (Don't answer your own question until later when he remembers to ask.)

**Actions**

1. Bring a favorite snack and a card to where he works. Announce in front of his coworkers, "Happy Husband Appreciation Day."

2. Take him on his favorite date (ball game, concert, etc.) as a surprise and tell him it's because you respect the man he is (or is becoming).

3. Reach across the breakfast/lunch/dinner table (yes, three times in the same day won't hurt) hold his hand and tell him one thing you respect about him.

## The Challenge of Control

In God's plan, the husband can't, in fulfilling his responsibility to God, be either a dictator or a doormat. His privilege is to become the lover of his wife. Instead of commanding her, he cherishes her. Instead of bossing, he blesses her. Instead of giving in or taking control, he gently controls the give and take. He stops trying to remake her and starts loving her. Again God in his wisdom designed the relationship according to the designed needs of the husband and wife. The wife needs to be loved.

"How do you know when you are loved?" The question was asked by a pastor in a staff meeting. The answers were interesting. Every woman indicated that if a person listens to her—really listens, she knows she is loved. Most men know this about women (even if we still don't hear well). But, the second response seemed somewhat new. The most common word the women used to describe the way to their hearts was "authenticity."

### Authentic love

Loving with authenticity involves reacting the way the *author* of love intended.

But, in a world plastered with slick and superficial sentimentalities, it's difficult to make out his handwriting on the wall. One of the most difficult struggles for me (Marty) as a teen was peeling away the plaster as I tried to figure out what the Apostle Paul meant when he said that a husband was required to *love* his wife the way "Christ loved the church" (Ephesians 5:25). When I asked one of the guys at church what Paul meant, he responded with, "Just make sure you wear the pants in the family." Although he couldn't explain what this meant, the way he lived taught me that "wearing the pants" was easy: All you had to do was boss your wife around.

Although I wasn't sure, his interpretation seemed to contradict Jesus Christ's example. So, I asked my youth pastor, Donn Mogford, and he explained that if I wanted to know what Paul meant, all I had to do was read the next part of the verse. When I did, I found this: "Husbands love your wives the way Christ loved the church *and gave himself up for her.*"

I had watched Pastor Donn hold his wife's hand as they chatted at the back of the church. I had heard him talk about her with deep respect. I had even seen him bring her red punch (was there any other kind?) at our church potlucks. "That's what Paul meant," I figured. I even observed this kind of behavior in my dad who, after committing himself to Bible study and prayer later in his life, bought my mom (a member of the Work-Your-Appendages-to-the-Bone club) a foot massage machine (kind of a modern twist to washing each other's feet, I think).

Their examples interpreted Paul's words clearly. The husband is to *give himself up*. Not give his leadership up. Not give his love up. But, give "himself" up. That truth has redeemed my marriage more than once.

### Authentic Love: Loving Your Wife

1. The next time a major event that your wife knows you "don't want to miss" comes along, surprise her and take her to do her favorite activity (yes, we're talking Super Bowl level here).

2. During your next conversation, ask if there's any childhood memory that she has thought about lately that has made her either happy or sad.

3. Adjust the mower height so you can carve her name in the front lawn. (Some wives like the humorous approach.)

These demonstrations of "giving yourself up" will speak to her understanding of authenticity.

When we fall in love and marry, we hope and pray that our love will always stay dreamlike, but then we wake up years or months later to the Beatles' "All the Lonely People" and we can't shut it off. The words play like a scratched CD over and over, haunting our failed hopes. When marriage feels this way, many couples head for the exits. They read the emotions like the credits at the end of a show and figure the movie's over. But, these relationships can be redeemed.

## MENDING MARRIAGE

There are eight steps that we recommend for resolving the relational conflicts that develop in a marriage. These steps are based on the primary causes: control issues and the missing ingredients of respect and love.

### Step 1: Understand the commitments of marriage

Our commitment to the person of Jesus Christ is what makes a Christian marriage different from any other. People become Christians by realizing they have sinned and can never meet God's standard (Romans 3:23). In missing the standard, the Bible says that they will spend eternity apart from God. But there is good news (that is what the word, "gospel," means). God loves us so much that he sent his Son, Jesus, to live a perfect life and die in our place. God accepted the sacrifice on our behalf and raised Jesus from the dead. By placing our faith in him and his pardon of our sin, we have eternal life and can be called Christians.

### *A focused commitment*

His forgiveness and his example move us to forgive and sacrifice in response to his love. There are times when I (Rich) take my attention off my wife, but as long as I don't take my focus off Jesus, he will remind me to pay attention to my relationship with LouAnna.

### An extreme commitment

It's unlikely that the wounds associated with the lack of control, respect, and authentic love in a marriage can heal without intense devotion. The greatest love stories ever known (including the greatest—the love of Jesus) have demonstrated total devotion. Lovers don't meet each other halfway. They give everything they have to give.

One of my (Marty's) favorite stories to tell at couples retreats concerns a cancer patient who created an account at a florist shop to cover the future expense of having flowers delivered to his wife for the rest of her life. Every year on Valentine's Day she received a bouquet of roses hand delivered by the shop owner. I tell that story, not to convince husbands to buy roses, but to remind them that even though the couple in the story endured the normal conflicts of marriage, he reached beyond the routines of normal husbands and demonstrated extreme commitment. Relationships rarely respond to less than wholehearted overtures.

### A growing commitment

Christian commitment is similar to WD-40, that all-purpose household lubricant. Once we spray it on, it starts eating away at the rusty areas of our lives, freeing us up to experience more of the wonder so tightly fastened to our Creator's love. One of the misconceptions of marriage is that, when people get married, they lose their individual identities. The opposite is true. "The goal in marriage is not to think alike, but to think together," says Robert C. Dodds. When we marry, our new relationship becomes a catalyst promoting growth that frees us to reach our potential. For the first time we have someone who is permanently in our court, encouraging us to give our best. Not only are we realizing our human potential, but we are becoming all that God wants us to become. If we don't allow commitment to eat through the rust and free the stubborn and self-centered aspects of our lives, we'll constantly face the dull grind of relational conflict—until the parts stop moving and the relationship rusts solid.

## Step 2: Check the current

Each summer the Rollinses and Trammells raft the Deschutes River. We put the Trammell boys in one raft and the adults in another. Even though the river is a slow, meandering current through the beautiful Oregon forest— and even though the boys are old enough to take care of themselves—we breathe less easy when they float out of sight. It starts with Linda asking, "Do you see the boys?" It infects LouAnna, who soon echoes, "Do you see the boys?" We paddle a little harder and look intently, relaxing only when they are once again in view.

Marriage is like being cast into a river. Our goal is to stay in touch. We never want to lose sight of each other. Some of us are cast into the slow currents and staying in touch is fairly easy. Others of us are cast into the rapids and, unless we work hard at it, we will quickly lose touch. Because the river flows insanely over the landscape of our lives, we are never guaranteed that our marriages will flow the way most men hope or most women dream. Staying in touch is the essence of a successful marriage. Hold each other daily. Eat together whenever possible. Use these times to check the current.

## Step 3: Couple your prayer

We have already included prayer as a necessary step in resolving conflict. We need wisdom and direction in every conflict, and God promises to give it freely and without reservation. When we list prayer in this context, we are emphasizing praying as a couple. Praying together not only accomplishes the same goals as personal prayer, but it draws the couple together in ways that no other activity can.

*The reported divorce rate among couples that pray together
is about one in ten thousand.*

Prayer is an intimate act before our Creator. When a
couple shares with God and each other their deepest
fears and thoughts about their marriage and the events
surrounding them, they add glue which further cements
their relationship. They gain heavenly support from
the God who invented marriage. They gain a mutual
understanding. Studies have indicated that in staying power,
praying separates the marriages that last from those that do
not. Dr. Phillip C. McGraw writes in his bestselling book,
*Relationship Rescue* :

> … an interesting statistic shared by David McLaughlin in
> his wonderful series entitled *The Role of the Man in the Family*
> reflects that the divorce rate in America is at a minimum one
> out of two marriages. But the reported divorce rate among
> couples that pray together is about one in ten thousand. Pretty
> impressive statistic, even if you reduce it a thousandfold.[3]

It *is* a pretty amazing statistic! We have discovered as
we have opportunities to meet with couples that those who
pray together have a greater strength and deeper intimacy.

### Step 4: End the stalemate

One of the common mistakes we make as couples is waiting.
We know what we want in a relationship. We also intuitively
know what our partner wants. We could give them what
they want, but usually don't until they give us what we want.
This stalemate produces more quarrels and dissatisfaction,
which produces a greater sense of estrangement. Common
sense should tell us that if we can't control the other
person and we can only control ourselves, we need to do
something—something other than wait for them to give us
what we want or need.

We see it all of the time as we meet with couples. The husband is waiting to be respected before he will love his wife. The wife is waiting to be loved before she will treat her husband with respect. The result is that no one gets much of anything from the marriage. Somebody has to give in. If that somebody is you and you are the wife, you should try reaching out to your husband using the ideas listed earlier in this chapter. Treat him with special respect.

If you are the husband, you need to reach out in tenderness and start loving her in a way she can understand. Instead of acting like you're entitled, start deserving her respect. Become the lover. Use the ideas mentioned earlier in this chapter and watch where they take you as a husband. It is amazing what happens when our wives start "feeling" loved. All of a sudden they begin to reciprocate.

## Step 5: Realize you can only change yourself

We are also reminded that we can change no one but ourselves. The irony has always been that, as soon as we begin changing, those around us begin changing, too. Looking back, I (Rich) realize that I fell in love with my wife because of her differences as well as our similarities. I wanted a wife who was unique; I did not want another me. I wanted her to become all that she could be. I discovered that when I loved her, she began to feel free to become that person. We still have conflict, but we have stopped trying to change each other.

## Step 6: Do it in love

Several years ago, Dr. Gary Chapman described five main love languages: "words of affirmation, quality time, receiving gifts, acts of service, and physical touch." If your love language is "giving gifts," you might assume that everyone is a gift-giver. But you may be married to a person who expresses his or her love with "words of affirmation." They

keep waiting for you to say something nice and you keep
waiting for a gift. Until you discover your love language,
you may be saying, "I love you," but the other person isn't
hearing it. Dr. Chapman gives us three steps to discovering
our love language.

1. What does your spouse do or fail to do that
   hurts you most deeply? The opposite of what
   hurts you most is probably your love language.

2. What have you most often requested of your
   spouse? The thing you have most often
   requested is likely the thing that would make
   you feel most loved.

3. In what way do you regularly express love to
   your spouse? Your method of expressing love
   may be an indication that that would also make
   you feel loved.[4]

*"It takes minutes to love the way someone makes you feel,
but years to feel the way they love."*
—Mark Goulston

The Apostle Paul is concerned with the character of
our love languages when he writes in the biblical book of 1
Corinthians,

Love is patient, love is kind. It does not envy, it does not boast,
it is not proud. It is not rude, it is not self-seeking, it is not
easily angered, it keeps no record of wrongs. Love does not
delight in evil but rejoices with the truth. It always protects,
always trusts, always hopes, always perseveres. Love never fails.
(1 Corinthians 13:4–8)

Paul's description moves love from the abstract to the quantifiable. Patience is measurable. Kindness is measurable. Paul's description of love removes our excuses for saying "I love you," but never showing it in what we do. Many of our conflicts would be readily resolved if love were added to the mixture.

## Step 7: Stop remembering

At some point, we need to stop opening up the photo albums of each other's failures and move on. We do that by forgiving. We will spend more time on this concept in chapter ten, but—simply said—if all we do is stare at the negatives in the photo album of our relationship, very little positive will develop. We need to stop remembering what shouldn't be dwelt on.

## Step 8: Work on being friends

Mark Goulston said, "Take action when you fall out of like and you won't fall out of love." [5] Being best friends with your spouse is an important facet of a rewarding relationship. The Apostle Paul exhorted his protégé, Titus, to instruct older women in the church to teach younger women how to love their husbands. The word he uses for "love" is the love of friendship. Paul wanted the women to be best friends with their husbands.

Our (Rich's and Marty's) best friends are our wives. Whenever we hear someone say that we should treat our family as friends and our friends as family, we think *that's easy—they're the same people!* Being friends means we have fun with each other, endure the truth from each other, and find our comfort in each other. That way, when the conflicts come, we can rest in the friendship created by years of working on them. We believe that every couple *can* learn to add one plus one and come up with only one. We can use the new math. We can learn to share the kind of oneness that annotates our anniversaries with candlelight and whispers.

As we're writing this book, we want you to know that we're working through these conflicts, too. And, we're praying that, like us, you will continue to find the encouragement and strength to redeem your relationships.

**BOLD IDEAS**

When we consider all of the opposing forces pitted against the modern marriage, it is a miracle that any marriage works.

All of a sudden we find ourselves in a foxhole fighting an enemy that remarkably resembles our spouse.

Understanding the definition of a Christian marriage helps us realign our marriage according to God's expectations.

A woman who is married to a jerk is best served if she doesn't respond like one.

Marriage is like being cast into a river. Our goal is to stay in touch.

Many of our conflicts would be readily resolved if love were added to the mixture.

## CHAPTER NINE

# SOLUTION

# WINNING THE WAR OF THE WORLDS

*A whole new generation of Christians has come up believing that it
is possible to "accept" Christ without forsaking the world.*
—A.W. Tozer

*What good is it for a man to gain the whole world,
and yet lose or forfeit his very self?*
—Jesus Christ

The minute I (Rich) hear the words of the old spiritual,
"This World Is Not My Home," the melody moves from my
head to my foot and it starts tapping to the rhythm. J. R.
Baxter's song captures a biblical truth: This isn't home for
us. As a kid, this song made sense to me in a sentimental
way. Growing up, I believed its message, but began to feel,
instead, like "Harry" in the Eagles hit song, "New York
Minute," who one day "crossed some line" and was "too
much in this world."[1]

When I came out of college, I was ready to make my
mark in health care, but ten years later, I looked around
and realized that I had crossed that line and "was too much

in this world." I had a great job, a spacious home, a good church, a Porsche—I thought I had it all. Through a series of events motivated by my love affair with the world, I faced losing my wife and family. A conversation with my pastor helped me realize I was at war with two worlds: the one on earth and the other in heaven. It was destroying my relationships. Worldliness does that.

## A Year in the Life of Mike and Andrea

This is the war that Andrea and Mike are battling as they pay bills in their study.

Tension packs the room as they revisit the enormity of their financial problem. Mike works as a middle manager in a growing high-tech company. But, after five years there, his $90,000 annual salary isn't enough to cover their expenses. Andrea works part time. She can't work any more without robbing time from their two young boys. Half of what she earns goes toward paying for day care.

Tonight is no different from all of the other taxing "bill nights." Mike says they're struggling because Andrea has a Macy's in her closet. She says it's more like a J. C. Penney from the last decade. She reminds him that playing golf is an expensive luxury. He defends his golf expenses as a good business move. When all of their bills are combined, they are $300 a month short. In the past, they refinanced their house to make up the difference. They now have no equity left, even though the house is worth nearly $200,000 more than the $650,000 they paid. Each month they put the $300 on a credit card. (They're accumulating air miles, but they can't afford to go anywhere.)

The solution temporarily resolves the cash flow problem, but the weight never leaves. They feel like all they're doing is switching heavy luggage from one hand to the other while hurrying through the airport of life. They discuss changing banks to get a lower interest rate. But, Mike and Andrea

know they need to switch more than hands and banks; they
need to switch worlds.

"Set your minds on things above, not on earthly things"
(Colossians 3:2 ).

Even though they are making more money than their
parents ever made, they fight more and laugh less. Their
financial frenzy has damaged their respect for each
other, so the tenderness is gone. Their two sons listen to
emotional outbursts almost every night. They've learned to
yell at each other and crave new toys just like Mom and
Dad. Mike and Andrea's unwillingness to get rid of the
country club membership and replace their new BMW with
an economical second car is motivated by questions like,
"What would people think?" That kind of question results
from losing what we call, "the war of the worlds."

"Dear friends, I urge you, as aliens and strangers in the world,
to abstain from sinful desires, which war against your soul" (1
Peter 2:11).

According to the Center for American Progress:

- The average American family's debt has
  increased over 30 percent between 2001 and
  2004. It presently stands at 108.4 percent of
  income.

- Approximately 13.5 percent of the families
  surveyed have debt-service expenses (monthly
  payments) that average 40 percent of their
  income.

- Families are having a hard time keeping up in
  the current economic climate. [2]

The problem is exacerbated by fast cash and credit cards. What we want, we can buy ... because our debt is invisible—until it ruins our relationships.

> "Life is more than food, and the body more than clothes" (Luke 12:23).

## Too much in this world

It is a complicated picture. This world system presents a standard of life that is far beyond the average person's means to achieve. The standard drags us beneath the surface of an unmerciful ocean of discontent whose relentless waves pound against the shores of our sanity, whispering, "more, more, more." We become depressed, and all hope for redeeming relationships damaged by this world's values sinks beneath waves of despair.

The Eagles capture this melancholic depression in their song "New York Minute." The song tells of a Wall Street broker, "Harry," whose clothing was found "scattered somewhere on the track." The song reminds us that men "get lost sometimes" and die because they live "too much in this world." It's a powerful reminder of what the apostle John meant when he said,

> If anyone loves the world, the love of the Father is not in him. For everything in the world—the cravings of sinful man, the lust of his eyes and the boasting of what he has and does—comes not from the Father but from the world. The world and its desires pass away, but the man who does the will of God lives forever (1 John 2:15–17).

## War wounds

John describes four wounds that pierce our relationships. First, we do not "love" God. Second, we "crave" more. Third, we "lust" after what we see around us. And fourth, we "boast" about what we have. Understanding these wounds helps us understand why any one of us can find ourselves on the same spreadsheet as Andrea and Mike.

### Love's lost

When we are "too much in this world," we miss out on fulfilling the joy of our created purpose. We miss out on the one relationship that makes all our relationships truly redemptive. If "the love of the Father is not in us," we won't have it to add warmth and meaning to our relationships, and we won't have it to help us heal the hurt of relationships damaged by a love of the world. What Andrea and Mike started with was every young person's hope for "real love." They never would have dreamed that their attraction could be turned from each other to a world of designer clothes, diamonds, and distractions.

### Curbing the cravings

Unfortunately, through a phenomenon educators call "transference," we've learned to treat our relationships the way we treat products. We carry over what we learn about consuming in our market economy into our friendships and relationships with family members, coworkers and employees. It becomes easy for us to focus our energies on what we crave rather than on what we can give. We crave a product; we crave a relationship. It just makes sense to us. But people aren't products. In a sense, the more we buy into this kind of lifestyle, the more we sell out on every relationship we have. How do we curb the cravings?

In my (Marty's) Mass Media class the students explore the contrast between the world view that says life is about consuming and the Scriptures that teach that life is about adoring God and giving to others. The goal is that, along with identifying the underlying media theories, the students will learn to examine the effects the war of the worlds has on who they have become. The discussion is designed to help students understand how adoration helps protect us from discontentment while giving protects us from the power of our cravings.

## Changing the Frequency: Curbing the Cravings

The following exercise can help you change the frequency of conflicts caused by being "too much in this world."

1. Divide a piece of paper into three columns.

2. In the first column, write a list of things you "crave" about God or your life as a Christian. At the end of each item put a number representing how many years you believe you have valued it (approximately).

3. In the middle column make a list of your ten most expensive purchases. At the end of each item, write when you purchased the item and when you began to be dissatisfied with it (approximately).

4. In the third column, list any recurring relational conflicts. Try to list them next to the item in the middle column that might have contributed to the conflict.

5. Ask God to create cravings for those things that have lasting value.

Mike and Andrea followed this counsel, and their relationship began to improve—but it wasn't easy. Powerful cultural influences continued to haunt their efforts.

## THE CULTURE OF CRAVE

Orson Wells' *War of the Worlds* radio drama introduced us to media's impact on our lives. Although current media may not be designed to produce panic the way the radio drama did, the billions of dollars that companies spend on advertising do impact our relationships. Here's an example.

In television, we have gone from the Dick Van Dyke show where the censors refused to show a bedroom with a double bed, to Victoria's Secret commercials that reveal more than the early issues of *Esquire* (a magazine for men). The ads work for the lingerie manufacturer, but not for our relationships. The truth is that as the media continue to show *more*, intimacy means less. The desire for *more* also tends to cause us to "crave" what we can't have, which causes us to miss out on what we do have. We have found that this is a major impetus for the boredom that eventually creates relational conflict. When we align our relationships with the world and its values, we begin to suffer from aspects of our "cravings" that do not promote either closeness or satisfaction.

Research shows that media industries and businesses have valid reasons to believe that, unless they keep us wanting *more*, we will stop paying attention to their commercials, programs, and products. When was the last time you saw a sitcom or movie about a character's success in learning to save money? How often do advertisers appeal to our self-control? In a market economy like ours, there is even greater potential that a relationship will be damaged by being "too much in this world."

> *"Onward Christian soldiers, marching as to war,*
> *Stopping at each shop, to buy a little more.*
> *Christ the Royal Master, leads against the foe,*
> *But with so much baggage, we're moving kind of slow."*
> —Ken Langley

## The Maze of Materialism

The Apostle John describes a third wound created by the war of the worlds. Strong desire ("lust of the eyes") drives many of us into a preoccupation with what we see around us. Although the reference can relate to anything we might "lust" after, for our purposes of discussing solutions for relational conflict, this section focuses on materialism. It affected Andrea and Mike and infects a large number of Americans, including many Christians. This thought is echoed by Jesus Christ when he taught that man cannot serve both God and money (Matthew 6:24). He will serve one or the other. Literally, the word translated "money" is a much broader term connoting material wealth. The point is that this world's wealth is tough to handle. It's a seductive and suffocating taskmaster.

When Mike was interviewed for his present position, he and Andrea began dreaming. They dreamed of making $45,000 more each year than the $45,000 Mike was presently making. They talked about the "fact" that they would no longer be middle class people. As a result, they needed to live like people who earned $90,000. Two cars, an expensive house, two trips to Hawaii, and a country club membership later, they wondered why they were fighting all of the time. Materialism pulled them away from each other, not because it caused them to "crave," but because it replaced their love for each other with a lust for things.

Materialism affects all of our relationships. A father and his son, a mother and her daughter, a worker and her colleagues—all are affected by its subtle control. Materialism drops us in a maze because its desires are connected and convoluted. One desire connects itself to another and, before we know it, our thoughts and waking dreams are almost entirely focused on the next purchase, not on the next person we meet. The maze of materialism leads to dead ends.

## BETTER BOASTS

It is embarrassing to admit, but I (Rich) know what the Apostle John means. When LouAnna and I owned a Porsche, I felt special. Honestly, I felt superior. I was a Porsche owner! When I got into LouAnna's station wagon, I was ordinary. When I slipped behind the wheel of this gleaming machine filled with exquisite leather, I felt like royalty. I became snooty. When I passed other Porsches, I would flash my lights. They would return the gesture in acknowledgment that we were a better class of people. As a Porsche owner, I acted like I was several steps above Ford and Chevy owners in the car chain (never mind the fact that I also owned a Ford station wagon).

I was a living example of the person John described as filled with the "lust of his eyes" and the "boasting of what he has and does." The superior attitude affected my friendships and family because I was on my way up and I didn't want anyone to slow me down. What turned me around? A simple comparison with something the Apostle Paul told the Galatian Christians:

"May I never boast except in the cross of our Lord Jesus Christ, through which the world has been crucified to me, and I to the world" (Galatians 6:14).

### Changing the Frequency: A Better Boast

Load this passage to the opening window of your PDA or tape it to your dashboard, mirror, or keyboard:

*May I never boast except in the cross of our Lord Jesus Christ, through which the world has been crucified to me, and I to the world* (Galatians 6:14).

This comparison made all the difference for me.

As God used this passage and others to convict me of my love for the world, I began to see the problem from God's perspective. LouAnna had always seen God's perspective on my Porsche (every time she fastened the seatbelt in her Ford station wagon). God used her to drive some sense into my thick skull.

Understanding the war of the worlds helps us understand the serious tone in James's biblical letter to the churches in Jerusalem.

> What causes fights and quarrels among you? Don't they come from your desires that battle within you? You want something but don't get it. You kill and covet, but you cannot have what you want. You quarrel and fight. You do not have, because you do not ask God. When you ask, you do not receive, because you ask with wrong motives, that you may spend what you get on your pleasures. You adulterous people, don't you know that friendship with the world is hatred toward God? (James 4:1–4)

According to James, when we love the world, we can expect fights and quarrels. They emanate from an inner battle in our hearts. What we need is a new reality—a new way of seeing things.

That's what Mike and Andrea desperately needed. Their life had degenerated into disdain for each other (a far cry from the delight at the wedding). With their debt continuing to grow, they had no hope. It all came to a head when Mike's Mom and Dad came to California to spend Christmas with them. The minute Mike's parents got settled in the house, they sensed that whatever was hanging in the air would take more than a few room deodorizers to fix.

> "For the love of money is a root of all kinds of evil. Some people, eager for money, have wandered from the faith and pierced themselves with many griefs" (1 Timothy 6:10).

While fixing pancakes the next morning, Andrea burst into tears. As the tears flowed, Jake and Martha slowly surrounded Andrea and held her as she poured out years of pent-up emotions and anxiety. Jake's forty years of pastoring people in similar situations had prepared them for the next steps.

That night when Mike walked in the living room, he sensed something was different. Mike's parents were sitting quietly staring at him as he entered.

"What's wrong?" he asked.

I wish that I could report that during the conversation, Jake and Martha's professional expertise put their kids' marriage back together, but the best they could do was get Mike to agree to attend church that Sunday.

It was the Sunday before Christmas and, when they walked into the building, they were reminded how pleasant it was to be in a church again. Mike noticed an insert in the bulletin that caught his attention. It asked, "Are you drowning in debt? Is it sucking the life out of your day? Come join us and find practical solutions."

Mike couldn't get the announcement out of his mind. As Christmas approached, he could think of nothing but that insert. He asked himself, "Could there be help?" The last year had been rough on everyone. They faced losing their house and cars. The country club had just assessed him an additional $10,000 for "renovations to the clubhouse and pool." He did not have the heart to show the letter to Andrea. It would be the final straw. He had no idea where the money would come from.

> "But mark this: There will be terrible times in the last days. [2]People will be lovers of themselves, lovers of money, boastful, proud ... " (2 Timothy 3:1–2).

The Saturday after Christmas, Jack and Martha were nearly finished getting ready for the trip to the airport. Jack quietly knocked at Mike's study door. When he opened the door, he was immediately struck with how much weight Mike had lost. He looked terrible, and his father's heart ached for his son. Jack crossed the room and placed an envelope on the desk. Mike looked at the envelope and then at his dad.

"What is it?"

"It's a gift from your mom and me. Before you open it, promise me that you will do what it enables you to do."

Mike promised and opened the envelope. There were two tickets to the financial workshop at the church. Mike had given up hope of going because he didn't know where he could find $125 needed for Andrea and him to attend. Now he was hoping she would still want to.

Mike and Andrea did attend, and it was the beginning of a new perspective and a renewed relationship. They learned a set of biblical priorities that helped them win this part of the war of the worlds. They also met Edwin and Liz, two singles who were also struggling with finances. One thing they had in common was their debt load. Together they learned that the first priority for redeeming their relationships was seeing the conflict from God's perspective.

## Priority 1: Get perspective

In his book, *The Man in the Mirror,* Patrick Morley suggests that there are two categories of Christians in the world. One he labels the "cultural Christian" and the other the "biblical Christian."

"Cultural Christianity means to pursue the God we want instead of the God who is ... wanting Him to be more of a gentle grandfather type who spoils us and lets us have our own way. ... It is wanting the God we have underlined in our Bibles without wanting the rest of Him, too. It is God relative instead of God absolute."[3]

"Cultural Christians" are really functional atheists. They profess a belief in God but live as if he were dead. They have the same goals as those who have never attended church or entered a living relationship with God.

Instead, God has called us to be "biblical Christians," men and women who reflect God's perspective on their surroundings. They are in the world, but live like nomads, "just a passing through." They may be wealthy or poor, but they give God the credit for everything he provides.

The Apostle Paul captured God's perspective when he cautioned the young pastor, Timothy, about contentment and wealth.

> But godliness with contentment is great gain. For we brought nothing into the world, and we can take nothing out of it. But if we have food and clothing, we will be content with that. People who want to get rich fall into temptation and a trap and into many foolish and harmful desires that plunge men into ruin and destruction. For the love of money is a root of all kinds of evil. Some people, eager for money, have wandered from the faith and pierced themselves with many griefs (1 Timothy 6:6–10).

The second priority the instructors introduced was called "Let's Get Spiritual."

### Priority 2: Get spiritual

Mike was asked to read aloud to the group at his table.

> So do not worry, saying, "What shall we eat?" or "What shall we drink?" or "What shall we wear?" For the pagans run after all these things, and your heavenly Father knows that you need them. But seek first his kingdom and his righteousness, and all these things will be given to you as well (Matthew 6:31–33).

The workbook chapter stressed the necessity of differentiating between wants and needs. Under the heading, "*Taking a self-evaluation,*" they found the following:

1. Why do you own what you own?

2. How many of your expenses are "wants" and how many are "needs"?

3. Is there any evidence in your checkbook that you serve God?

4. Are you living beyond your means because of impulse spending?

5. Do you overspend because you're concerned about what people think?

6. How much time do you spend arguing and worrying about finances?

7. Do you drive a car that is reliable or are you making a statement?

8. Do you have money to help someone in a time of need?

9. Are you a "cultural" or a "biblical" Christian?

10. Do you pray about your spending?

After going through the list, they were asked to discuss their answers with others in the group. They chose Edwin and Liz. They were all amazed at how similar their answers were. After a short break, they were asked to rate the following statements on a scale of 1–10, with 1 meaning "not important" and 10 meaning "very important."

- I want to gain financial freedom from the burden of debt.
- I want to see God back in my life.
- I want to set spiritual priorities in my life.
- I am willing to get serious.

The instructor said that if anyone scored these questions "8" or higher, he or she needed to turn to "Priority 3." They all turned to the next page.

## Priority 3: Get serious

The instructor read 1 John 2:15–17 and James 4:1–10. Most had read these verses before, years ago, but they never understood them like they did with this reading. "Love not the world … What causes arguments and quarrels?"

"It sure describes us." Mike thought. Then the instructor outlined ten commands.

> Submit yourselves, then, to God. Resist the devil, and he will flee from you. Come near to God and he will come near to you. Wash your hands, you sinners, and purify your hearts, you double-minded. Grieve, mourn and wail. Change your laughter to mourning and your joy to gloom. Humble yourselves before the Lord, and he will lift you up (James 4:7–10).

Mike was moved by the last command. He had never seen humility as a strength. He was proud of his education, job, country club membership, BMW, 5-bedroom house, beautiful wife, and good looks. Mike knew that his country club membership was important to him only because, of the dozen or so people who were at his level at work, he was the only one who belonged to a club. It happened to be the same club that his boss belonged to. Being a member made Mike feel like he was more successful than his coworkers.

> *"There is no calamity greater than lavish desires.*
> *There is no greater guilt than discontentment.*
> *And there is no greater disaster than greed."*
> —Lao-Tzu

Mike tried to maintain his composure and was fine until they were asked to spend some time in prayer with their partner. As Mike and Andrea sat in a secluded corner of the conference center, Mike began to sob. Andrea never realized they shared the same fears and pain. As they returned to their table, they felt hope for the first time in years.

## Reality: They needed a new paradigm

We live our lives according to a set of expectations and perceptions. These formulate our paradigm for life. Mike and Andrea had adopted the world's paradigm for life and success. It was contrary to the biblical paradigm for Christians who live their lives for the glory of God.

## Reality: They needed the peace of God's provision

When I (Rich) moved my family from California to Salem, Oregon in 1978, a new chapter began in our lives. We had always believed that God was our provider, but it had been years since we had experienced it firsthand. I left an impressive job that included a great salary, eight weeks vacation, several weeks of educational leave, a life insurance policy, and a disability insurance policy—all provided at no cost to us.

We knew that moving to Salem was going to be financially difficult, but we had no idea what that could mean. Within several months, we faced the possibility that the college where we now served might close. Enrollment was down, cash flow was a disaster. The loss of more than 60 percent of our previous income was made worse by the prospect that even the small amount we were being paid might not be paid at all.

Yet as we look back on that time, we marvel at God's faithfulness. We never missed a bill or a meal. Who meets *your* needs—the world or God?

## Reality: We need to live within God's provision

Each of us has the same decision: Will we live within our means or beyond them? It is a mistake to think that God is obligated to give us all we want. He meets our needs and provides through our jobs and other means the resources we need to live. We must wisely choose needs over wants.

## Reality: Wealth is often the American's test of spiritual maturity

> "On the first day of every week, each one of you should set aside a sum of money in keeping with his income, saving it up, so that when I come no collections will have to be made" (1 Corinthians 16:2).

Mike had seen his parents tithe all of his life. Why should he give $9,000 annually to some church to spend? If he did, how would he pay his country club dues? What he didn't realize was that his lack of giving was a measure of his spiritual maturity. Giving is a big issue in the American church because we worship money. At the church where I (Rich) serve, if a person doesn't give, they cannot serve in leadership. That offends many, but it never offends the spiritually mature.

## Reality: You can't do it alone

The changes started when Andrea was willing to confess to her in-laws Jake and Martha that their marriage was in trouble. The changes continued at a workshop that Mike's mom and dad paid for. The workshop leaders introduced them to the problem from a biblical perspective. God used the Bible to begin convicting them about their love for the world. They made some new best friends. The point is they didn't do this alone. It took others.

## EPILOGUE

It's been a year since Mike and Andrea attended the financial workshop. Mike changed jobs. It became clear to him that the goals of the company would not fit his new ones. He sold his country club membership for a $28,000 profit! They paid off one of the cars and gave up the second one. This allowed them to save the house. His new job pays well, but $10,000 less than his other job. Valley Church has become the center of their family life. Mike and Andrea are well on their way—because, like the old spiritual says, they're "not at home in this world anymore."

**BOLD IDEAS**

Our debt is invisible—until it ruins our relationships.

When we align our relationships with the world and its values, we begin to suffer from aspects of our "cravings" that do not promote either closeness or satisfaction.

It becomes easy for us to focus our energies on what we crave rather on what we can give.

The maze of materialism leads to dead ends.

What we need is a new reality—a new way of seeing things.

"Cultural Christians" are really functional atheists.

We live our lives according to a set of expectations and perceptions. These formulate our paradigm for life.

Who meets *your* needs—the world or God?

## CHAPTER TEN

SOLUTION

# DEALING WITH DAMAGED TRUST

*Forgiveness*
*Is the mightiest sword*
*Forgiveness of those you fear*
*Is the highest reward*
*When they bruise you with words*
*When they make you feel small*
*When it's hardest to take*
*You must do nothing at all.*

—Charlotte Bronte

She sat at the kitchen table fingering the note and staring at yesterday's warmed-over coffee. She replayed her marriage, pausing at scenes that didn't make sense. As she spliced the scenes together, the pattern of Gene's lies began to lay itself out on the oily film in her mug. It seemed so clear now. She focused on a period of several months when the phone rang three or four times a day, but there was never anyone there. She thought it was strange that whomever it was had blanked out his or her Caller ID, but she assumed it was a still just a "wrong number."

She remembered frequently smelling perfume on Gene's suit coats. When she asked, Gene reminded her that his office was filled with women. "My new secretary, Mary, usually puts my coat away for me," he'd suggested. "It must be her perfume."

Beth paused her memory on a day she surprised Gene in his office. She'd almost asked Mary about hanging Gene's coat up, but felt guilty about even questioning Gene's honesty. Beth thought she always gave Gene the benefit of the doubt because she had no reason to question his commitment; now she wondered if she gave him the benefit because she was afraid she'd find what now stared at her from the note in her trembling hand. The note apologized for "the hurt she had caused" and warned that Gene had "been unfaithful" more than a few times. The note was signed, "Sue."

> *"A good marriage is at least 80 percent good luck in finding the right person at the right time. The rest is trust."*
> —Nanette Newman

Beth's memory paused at a scene in the mall where a year ago she'd accused him of visually undressing a clerk in Macy's. She was embarrassed and hurt. He again professed his commitment to her but added that "it didn't hurt to look at the menu, even if you were on a diet." She'd never understood that comparison. It made her feel like a salad in a steak house. But, not wanting to create a scene, she'd let it go. She'd let a lot of things go.

She played back the audio of confusing conversations with mutual friends, even her newest friend, Sue. She remembered asking Gene, "Why do things feel so awkward? What do they know about us that we don't know?" What she didn't realize then was Gene knew the answers to those questions. Now she did, too! After a box of Kleenex, she called Sue. Sue answered on the first ring, before Beth could change her mind.

"Hello?"

Some coffee splashed onto the table. Before she could shut the phone off, she heard herself stammer, "It's Beth ... I just read your note." The words stopped. She couldn't swallow. She hoped Sue would break the silence, and she did, with long, uneven sobs. Finally, they shortened and straightened out a bit.

"I'm so sorry, Beth. ... can you ever forgive me?"

Beth wanted to scream and cry at the same time. But only tears came—until she felt the first breezes of hate. The hatred felt good, even right. At first, it gave her strength as it dried her tears like a hot desert wind, protecting her from the pain. But all at once the hate was choked by something deep and desperate—something that labored through the subterranean passages of her heart. Beth knew what it was: Somehow she felt remorse for Sue—an unwelcomed remorse.

"I can't talk now." She turned off the phone and shoved it next to the mug.

> *"Physical infidelity is the signal, the notice given,*
> *that all fidelities are undermined."*
> —Katherine Anne Porter

Gene came home to his personal belongings thrown into boxes and dumped on the front porch. Taped conspicuously to one of the boxes was Sue's letter to Beth and another note.

> Gene, you don't live here anymore. Our marriage is over. Please leave me and the children alone. I called your parents and told them everything.
>
> *—Beth*

Gene was devastated. He had never considered the consequences of Beth finding out. He packed his SUV and sat in the driveway. Tears rolled down his cheeks as the full impact of what he had done sank in.

After three weeks of separation, Gene and Beth agreed to try to save their marriage. Their neighbor had attended a couples conference at which Linda and I (Marty) had spoken and, on the neighbor's advice, they called us for couples counseling. They decided that if their marriage could be repaired, it would take more than professional help—it would take a miracle.

During the first session together, Gene confessed his unfaithfulness and asked Beth for forgiveness. Linda and I watched the transformation. With mercy only God understands, Beth forgave him. After several more weeks of separation, Gene moved back into the home. But, a month later, he sat in my office again.

## THE TEST OF TRUST

"I don't believe she's forgiven me," he sighed. I listened as he rehearsed the inquisition that "trapped" him—the inquisition I reminded him he'd earned. "I just can't live like this," he countered. "She's always checking up on me. Why can't she forgive me?"

The truth was that Beth had forgiven him, but Gene had confused forgiveness with trust. The two are not the same. Two people can forgive each other without trusting each other. Trust has to be re-earned. If a couple like Beth and Gene never trust again the marriage can survive, but it can't thrive. Trust is the catalyst that makes all the emotions and experiences of friendship intense and meaningful. Trust ignites embers and emblazons passion. Trust takes a spouse's attributes and holds them up before the world and exclaims, "This is my friend. This is someone I love." When trust is damaged, the delights of marriage diminish. And they won't come back—not even with forgiveness—if trust continues to labor under the weight of suspicion. What we have found in our counseling and study is that forgiveness is a gift, but trust has to be earned.

## Every relationship requires trust

The conflicts created by a lack of trust are not restricted to marriage. Distrust leads many managers to doubt an employee's ability to perform. "Micro-manage" was added to the dictionary because it gave a name to the universal sentiment employees share when they don't feel their bosses trust them. You may be experiencing this kind of conflict at work.

Trust also affects parents and children. If a parent has shared a child's secret with a friend or embarrassed a child in a social setting, it's difficult for the child to trust that parent and respond in a way that improves their relationship. It also becomes difficult for the child to trust in any new relationship. Trust has to be relearned.

Teens are often too young to realize that manipulation and exaggeration can damage the trust relationship with their parents. Getting home a few minutes late isn't a problem for most parents if the teen's track record is outstanding. However, if there are some holes in the track (like manipulation and hyperbole), the level of trust has lowered, and a "few minutes late" can create major conflict.

When forgiveness and trust are lacking in a relationship, it is difficult to resolve most conflicts because unfinished business keeps squeezing its way into our thinking and conversations. If two people are going to truly resolve their differences, they must finish the business. Without forgiveness, they may keep throwing past mistakes at each other rather than seriously seeking solutions.

*"To be trusted is a greater compliment than to be loved."*
—George MacDonald

George MacDonald was an inspiration to C. S. Lewis. The symbolism in his stories of romance in the hills of Scotland helped Lewis create his magical world of Narnia and the bestselling *The Lion, the Witch, and the Wardrobe.* MacDonald's view on this matter was that trust was a compliment someone earned through establishing strong character. He wrote, "To be trusted is a greater compliment than to be loved." In a world that reduces love to sentiment or sensuality, trust is undervalued. But trust is important because, in the process of resolving a conflict with a coworker, family member, or friend, we must entrust our thoughts and feelings. We will do this only if we trust the other person. This was a lesson Gene was learning.

## FORGIVENESS

Gene was right about the importance of forgiveness. So was Beth. The Bible commands forgiveness. The Apostle Paul wrote to the church of Ephesus,

> "Be kind and compassionate to one another, forgiving each other, just as in Christ God forgave you" (Ephesians 4:32).

### Forgiveness involves kindness and compassion

The Apostle Paul reminds us that forgiveness involves kindness and compassion. It's easy to be kind and compassionate to good friends; it's nearly impossible to express kindness and compassion to those who have harmed a loved one. That is why God gives the believer his own Holy Spirit, to live and work within the Christian's life. He is in the business of doing the impossible. Without kindness and compassion, forgiveness becomes pity. To be kind and compassionate to those who do not deserve it is fulfilling the command of Jesus to love our enemies. Jesus was not talking about having warm feelings towards our enemies. He was saying that we need to love them the way God does.

> *"When you forgive, you in no way change the past—*
> *but you sure do change the future."*
>
> —Bernard Meltzer

## We can't truly forgive until we've experienced God's forgiveness

The world looks at Christians and wonders how we can lose so much and still love others. It is because we have been forgiven much. There is a great story in the seventh chapter of the Gospel of Luke about an event in the life of Jesus. The Jewish religious leaders of the day, the Pharisees, were fascinated with Christ's swelling popularity and wanted some of it. One day a Pharisee named Simon invited Jesus to his home. They met with many others in what must have been an open courtyard. A woman who was known for her shameful life heard that Jesus was going to be there and showed up as an uninvited guest. She worked her way through the crowd until she stood immediately behind the Lord.

As Jesus spoke, she cried. Her tears of repentance fell on his feet. When she noticed the mess she was making, she began drying his feet with her hair. Moved by his message, character, and her growing belief in his divinity, she began to pour ointment on his feet and kiss them. Simon saw this and said to himself, "If this man were a prophet, he would know who is touching him and what kind of woman she is—that she is a sinner."

Jesus looked at him and asked a question. If two men each owed a financier money, one owing the equivalent of 500 days' wages and the other fifty days' wages, and both of their debts were forgiven, which one would love the financier the most? Simon correctly answered: the one with the biggest debt. Jesus reminded him that the woman had treated him with more love and respect than Simon had. Jesus finished his observations with the statement, "But he who has been forgiven little loves little" (Luke 7:47).

*"The glory of Christianity is to conquer by forgiveness."*
—William Blake

Simon believed he was better than the woman. In reality, he was no different—none of us is. We are that woman. The Apostle Paul reminded the Church at Colossae that "When you were dead in your sins ... God made you alive with Christ. He forgave us all our sins (Colossians 2:13).

It's hard to imagine anyone forgiving the way Christ forgave without having experienced God's forgiveness in Christ. When we accept this forgiveness, understanding how much we did not deserve it, we begin to understand how to forgive others. We understand that forgiveness is not based on being worthy.

*"I imagine one of the reasons people cling to their hates so stubbornly is because they sense, once hate is gone, they will be forced to deal with pain."*
—James Baldwin

### Forgiveness doesn't journal

Many years ago Alice came into my (Rich's) office carrying a notebook. She had scheduled time with me to help her in a failing marriage. After exchanging pleasantries, I asked how I could help. She opened a journal in which she had documented, in great detail, all her husband's faults. After twenty minutes, I interrupted.

"Alice, why are you here?" I asked.

"I want to solve the problems in my marriage," she said.

"I have the beginnings of a solution."

"You'll talk to Sam for me?"

"Probably later, but the first step doesn't involve him."

"Doesn't involve him? ... But he's the problem!"

"No, Alice, right now you are the problem."

Alice shot out of her seat so fast she dropped her journal. As she bent down to retrieve it, she tripped on her purse strap and fell into the couch. Now she was angry and embarrassed.

I asked again, "Alice, why did you come today?"

Over the next hour, we talked about forgiveness. Alice had never forgiven her husband. Yes, he was a jerk and, yes, he needed to change, but there was little hope without her willingness to forgive. The "jerk journals" documented his sins—and hers.

> *"A wise man will make haste to forgive,*
> *because he knows the true value of time,*
> *and will not suffer it to pass away in unnecessary pain."*
> —Samuel Johnson

## Forgiveness is up to us

Like so many of us, Alice was waiting for her husband to change before she forgave him. Forgiveness was not about him, however; it was about her. It is a mistake to think that forgiveness is based on the other person confessing or suffering enough. It is not necessary that the other person even know that he or she has offended. Many children of deceased parents believe they can't forgive their parents because the parents can't acknowledge the forgiveness. Yet forgiveness can be granted even to the dead.

Jesus Christ's close disciple, Peter, asked Jesus, how many times he must forgive—thinking seven times would be enough. Jesus answered, "I tell you, not seven times, but seventy-seven times" (Matthew 18:22). Forgiveness is not about the offender. It's about the person wronged. Alice never forgave, and her unwillingness led to a bitterness that blasted a cold chill through any warmth Sam tried to kindle. Their marriage lasted until the last child left for college. Alice filed for divorce and moved to another state. By then she probably had to rent a moving truck just for her journals! The sad thing is they're probably the only memories of Sam that traveled with her.

## Forgiveness is unnatural and seems unfair

One of the reasons Alice never forgave her husband is because forgiveness is not natural to us. It seems so unfair. Forgiveness is the intermediary act of love. It bridges the gap between condemned hope and restored relationship. Fairness is removed from the equation when we realize that forgiveness turns the unfairness of the treatment we received over to a competent Master, God. When we forgive, we turn things over to the only One who can fix them.

## Forgiveness is not a pardon

Forgiveness doesn't erase the debt we owe. We might forgive a criminal, but that doesn't mean a judge will take away the consequences. Forgiveness frees us to live in peace while it places the offender in the hands of a sovereign God.

## Forgiveness is not forgetting

Some years ago I (Marty) met with a couple who had discovered that their daughter was bulimic. They uncovered the problem by keeping a record of her excuses for missing meals, for calling in sick to work, for her reoccurring irritableness, as well as unusual (binge-type) food purchases on her credit statements. Over time, by piecing together these events, they were able to identify a pattern that led them to the possibility that their daughter was struggling with an eating disorder. The records they kept are gone now, but if each time they forgave an offense they had forgotten it, they might have missed helping her. Although we may forget an offense, forgiveness is not forgetting.

## Forgiveness is an act of faith

One of the unique characteristics of Christianity is the belief that God is in control. We believe that he sees everything and doesn't miss the bad things that others do to us. Because we believe this, we are able to move away from revenge. Christians are cautioned not to "get even" as the world might.

> Do not repay anyone evil for evil. Be careful to do what is right in the eyes of everybody. If it is possible, as far as it depends on you, live at peace with everyone. Do not take revenge, my friends, but leave room for God's wrath, for it is written: "It is mine to avenge; I will repay," says the Lord. On the contrary: If your enemy is hungry, feed him; if he is thirsty, give him something to drink. In doing this, you will heap burning coals on his head (Romans 12:17–20).

God sees the heart and motives, and his justice is always fair. One of the reasons we can forgive is because we have faith that God is a better judge than we could ever be.

## Forgiveness frees us

We will never be able to find compassion and kindness in our hearts towards those who have wronged us until we let the grievance go. Once we let it go, a burden is lifted and we begin to experience life again. One of the reasons Alice had stopped living was because she was tethered by the burden of years of abuse. The abuse had become an anchor holding her fast in the breakwater of bitterness. If she would have forgiven her husband, she would have experienced the freedom to love again. Even if her marriage eventually wrecked, she could have experienced some degree of respite and vibrancy.

> *"To forgive is the highest, most beautiful form of love.*
> *In return, you will receive untold peace and happiness."*
> —Robert Muller

## Forgiving is not the same as trusting

If a person borrows your car and has an accident which destroys the car, you can forgive him. The next time he asks to borrow the car, because you have forgiven him, you can still hand him the keys. If he has another accident, you can forgive him, but you probably will not give him the keys the next time he asks. Although he's been forgiven, you no longer trust him. The first crash was an incident. The second was the beginning of a pattern. Once the pattern surfaced, your trust disappeared. Forgiveness is free. Trust is earned.

When Gene said that Beth had not forgiven him, he was confusing forgiveness and trust. Gene wanted to resume the relationship as if his infidelity had never happened. He didn't understand that his wife had forgiven him, but too much had happened for her to trust him. He needed to re-earn her trust.

> *"It is better to suffer wrong than to do it,*
> *and happier to be sometimes cheated than not to trust."*
> —Samuel Johnson

As Linda and I (Marty) met with Gene and Beth, we explained that their marriage would never succeed without forgiveness and trust. Beth's response boarded up the windows and locked the doors. "I don't see how I could ever trust him again. Not in a million years!" In the following months, her lack of trust (motivated by his unwillingness to do whatever it took to re-earn it) slammed down the receiver and permanently disconnected their lives.

## A fable of forgiveness

Two friends were walking across a desert. As they discussed various views, the one friend, in anger, slapped the other. Startled and hurt, the friend kneeled and wrote in the sand, "Today my best friend slapped me." As they walked on they arrived at an oasis and began swimming in a deep pool; the friend who had been slapped began to drown. His friend reached into the pool and saved his life. The friend again kneeled, but this time he took great effort to carve into stone the words, "Today my best friend saved my life." Curious, the friend who had both slapped and saved his friend asked, "Why did you write in sand when I slapped you and in stone when I saved you?" The other friend stood to his feet, put his hand on his friend's shoulder and replied, "In my journey through this life I have learned that when your best friend does something kind, you should write it in stone so that the memory cannot fade. And, if he wounds you, you should write it in sand, so that the winds of time can blow it away."

I still believe that if Gene had promised to do whatever it took to re-earn Beth's trust and Beth had written a little more in the sand, their relationship could have been redeemed.

## REDEEMING DAMAGED TRUST

If you are experiencing conflict with a coworker, an employer, a spouse, a friend, or in a business partnership, you can repair the relationship or at least reduce the frequency of conflict. Let us suggest some action points.

## Don't ignore the red flags

If you asked Beth what she would have done differently in her relationship with Gene, she probably would have said,

"I wouldn't ignore all the clues about Gene's unfaithfulness." I (Rich) have a theory that says that if you ignore the red flags, they become banners. It took a banner in the form of a letter to open Beth's eyes.

### Don't react, respond

Beth could have reacted and divorced Gene. Fortunately, she didn't. She thought it through and asked him to move out instead. Had she not responded, Gene would have been tempted to continue to play his games (and with his track record, he probably would have yielded to temptation again). Reacting creates wounds that make resolution even more difficult. Don't react (unless someone's safety is at stake).

### Forgive

Some people carry the baggage of resentment and bitterness so long, they can't unpack it. They are miserable. There is only one solution: forgiveness. We forgive and forgive until the baggage is loaded onto the next train out of town. Since we've already covered the need for forgiveness earlier in the chapter, let's look at how to forgive.

- **Name it:** You can't forgive something you can't identify. It may be painful to admit how your trust was damaged, but you have to name it to forgive it.

- **Admit your part:** Many spouses of alcoholics admit later that they enabled the drinking. What is your part in the damaged trust?

- **Give it to God:** An authentic plea will bring all of God's assistance and power.

- **Throw it away:** I (Rich) ask people to write the offense down and throw it in the garbage can. "Now it's gone," I explain. "Don't dig it out."

- **Trade in your thoughts:** The Apostle Paul told the church in Philippi to think about things that are true, noble, right, pure, lovely, and admirable (Philippians 4:8). Trade your bitterness for these thoughts.

## RETOOL YOUR TRUST

Trust is built one behavior at a time. It will not return unless the one building it uses the tools of authenticity, honesty, and vulnerability. If we are serious about retooling, trust can remodel the relationship. There's no shortcut when it comes to redeeming relationships ruined by damaged trust.

### If you demolished the trust

- **Chisel your confession.** Confession isn't being sorry you got caught. It's chiseling painfully into stone your admission that the damage was your fault. It's admitting everything, not just the things others have already discovered.

- **Hammer out an honest apology.** Be specific about what you did. "I'm sorry I hurt you" doesn't hit the nail on the head. "I damaged your trust when I _____" is honest.

- **Draft a blueprint of what you will change.** If you are apologizing to a coworker, clearly identify how your behavior will change.

- **Dig deeper.** We must expend the extra effort. "What can I do to start back on the path to making things right?" is an honest response.

- **Hand over the permits.** We need to give the one we've offended permission to check up on all of our words and actions.

- **Relinquish the schedule.** Giving the other person the time he or she needs (or even wants) is the least we can do. The damage was our fault.

- **Miter the martyr.** We need to cut out all attempts to recast events in our favor. It's not about us. It's about the one we've wounded.

## If your trust was demolished

- **Forge Forgiveness.** Cool your anger quickly. Forgive as Jesus Christ forgave. He didn't make us suffer and sweat before giving us his unconditional forgiveness.

- **Inspect with kindness.** When you inspect the person's honesty, do it with kindness. It is not necessary that he or she knows each time you check.

- **Measure the progress.** Letting the one who's seeking to reestablish trust see where they are on the tape measure will encourage progress.

- **Hand over the tools.** As you begin to see progress, hand over the tools listed above one at a time.

## Start Over

Couples we have watched retool their relationships will tell you they feel like they've started all over. They've changed the way they relate to each other and things feel fresh and new. Even in corporate conflicts where trust has been damaged, coworkers find that retooling helps them rebuild. The offending party often experiences a deeper loyalty after being forgiven. Sometimes, after a few years, they even become the "go-to individual" because their trust has been thoroughly reestablished. When we get to the point where a new, more transparent way of relating is emerging, we need to put the past away—we need to start over.

*"It takes one person to forgive, it takes two people to be reunited."*
—Lewis B. Smedes

Rebuilding trust can be time-consuming like remodeling a home stud by stud. But, although it sounds one-dimensional, the result is sometimes better than the original. Family members, coworkers, and spouses we have worked with over our combined fifty years of ministry can tell you first hand. Our prayer is that you won't give up like Gene, that you won't keep "jerk journals" like Alice, and that you'll follow the blueprints inspired by our Creator. Ultimately, like any satisfying building project, you get what you pay for. The price here is forgiveness and a willingness to rebuild the trust that was damaged. Those two sacrifices will not only reflect the will of the master Carpenter, they'll redeem your relationships.

### Changing the Frequency: Conflict Created by Damaged Trust

Most damaged trust is created by too much trust. If you have continually experienced relationships damaged by trust, the following procedure can help:

1. Look at the personalities of the people with whom you have relationships and ask yourself what their greatest areas of weakness might be. Use the list in Galatians 5:19–21. (It comes before the popular "Fruit of the Spirit" passage and can help you contrast beneficial behaviors with those that damage trust.)

2. Pray for those areas and ask God to help you grow in sensitivity to the red flags that would indicate potential danger for the people around you.

3. After a few weeks in new relationships, ask the individuals if they "need" anything from you in order to work more effectively (work relationships), use their gifts more beneficially (church relationships), or be better friends. Simply asking the question will build a sense of trust between the two of you and make you more alert to their weaknesses.

4. Finally, although you don't want to become an overly suspicious person, set a week aside on your calendar. During that week, start each morning with an evaluation of any potential events that might lead to damaged trust.

This procedure can help you experience less pain in your relationships and reduce the frequency of conflicts that come from damaged trust.

BOLD IDEAS

Two people can forgive each other without trusting each other.

The world looks at Christians and wonders how we can lose so much and still love others. It is because we have been forgiven much.

Forgiveness is the intermediary act of love.

Forgiveness is not forgetting.

One of the unique characteristics of Christianity is the belief that God is in control.

Trust and respect don't automatically emerge in a damaged relationship without a plan. Time may heal, but trust needs evidence.

If you ignore the red flags, they become banners.

You have to name it to be able to forgive it.

Trust is built one behavior at a time.

CHAPTER ELEVEN

SOLUTION

# USING YOUR HEAD AND HEART

*I argue very well. Ask any of my remaining friends.*
*I can win an argument on any topic, against any opponent.*
*People know this, and steer clear of me at parties.*
*Often, as a sign of their great respect, they don't even invite me.*
—Dave Barry

Unlike like the facetious Dave Barry, most of us *want* to be invited to the party. Most of us want to be the kinds of people others enjoy being around. We want to sail through life cheering people on to love and good deeds, encouraging their dreams and leading them around the buoys of disappointment. What we don't *want* is to be the person who comes crashing down on their party like a sneaker wave. After all, we tell ourselves, we're made for riding waves, not making them. Often when we see conflict grinding in like an Oregon swell, we run for higher ground—to statements like "real love doesn't confront, it forgives"; "my relationships can succeed without confrontation"; "it's easier to put up with conflict." But, as we pointed out in chapter one, redeeming relationships involves busting the myths.

## Conflict Resolution Styles to Avoid

We've read the books and met the people. Some suggest that the best way to handle conflict is to adopt one strategy you can use for all situations, a one-size-fits-all approach. Just like those clothes that don't often fit (and leave much to be desired in the shape department), the one size conflict clothes don't fit either. Here are some to purge from your closet:

### Denial

"Conflict is simply a matter of overemphasizing your culture's or church's stereotypes. If you don't acknowledge it, it can't affect you." Just ask Marge and Nathan. They chanted their way into this strategy of denial almost forty years ago. And their conflicts have been minimal it seems—at least to them. Ask their children and friends, however, and it's a matter of mistaken identity. Marge and Nathan don't get along. But, like an alcoholic who can "stop whenever he wants," their relational conflict shows up everywhere except in their own heads. Their kids see it. Their few remaining friends see it, but Marge and Nathan deny its existence. Along with the hurt they create in the people around them, individuals who deny their conflicts enjoy less meaningful relationships and experience less life-satisfaction. They live less. They diminish the rewards of relationships because they cannot redeem a brokenness that isn't "real."

### Giving in

Some of us just give in when faced with conflict. People around us even encourage our "go with the flow" attitude when we let them have their way. Some of the time our areas of relational conflict are not important—like who chooses the next movie. But when a potentially difficult conflict arises, we pay an emotional price if we give in. Over time, our "give-in" attitude just plain gives out, and we become resentful and bitter.

## Stuff it

We've all lived, played, or worked with stuffers. When asked how they "feel," they go silent. Since it takes considerable emotional energy to share their feelings, they stuff them. They expect people to read their minds. Over time, they become angry and bitter—especially if our ESP is DOA. When it comes to avoiding conflict and enjoying relationships, they don't have the right stuff.

## Work a deal

The solutions that emerge from this approach are more about gaining some and losing little than about finding the best solution. The problem with working a deal is that the results may be based upon salesmanship (think "House of Representatives") where hidden agendas win the day, but discourage relationships tomorrow. With this strategy, people walk away placated, only to realize later that very little changed.

## The power play

In ice hockey, when a member of a team fouls a member of the opposing team, the player who committed the foul spends time in the penalty box. Then the other team has a one-person advantage called the "power play." Because the penalized team is one player short, the other team tries to take advantage of the situation.

When we use this approach in conflict management, we are usually trying to set up the conflict resolution situation so that we have an advantage. Instead of letting the other person use all his or her players (like the place we meet, the topics we allow, the time of day, the evidence we reject) we use the power play so that we have more players on the ice. But the problem with resolving conflict with this approach is it never redeems the relationship—it never gets off the ice.

## USING OUR HEARTS AND HEADS

True resolution takes a servant's heart, a loving manner, a listening ear, and an openness to communicate effectively. It takes maturity—and that's, partly, a head skill.

### The servant's head

We hear a lot about the "servant's heart," but what about his head? It's what the rest of this chapter is about.
The servant considers the following:

### *Own your own behavior*

The Bible has much to say about controlling our behavior.

> Finally, all of you, live in harmony with one another; be sympathetic, love as brothers, be compassionate and humble. Do not repay evil with evil or insult with insult, but with blessing, because to this you were called so that you may inherit a blessing. For, "Whoever would love life and see good days must keep his tongue from evil and his lips from deceitful speech. He must turn from evil and do good; he must seek peace and pursue it. For the eyes of the Lord are on the righteous and his ears are attentive to their prayer, but the face of the Lord is against those who do evil" (1 Peter 3:8–12).

Did you notice the behavior the biblical author is supporting?

- Live in harmony.
- Be sympathetic.

- Love.

- Be compassionate.

- Be humble.

- Don't get into a verbal knife-throwing contest.

- Control your mouth.

- Seek peace.

The first rule in resolving conflict is to control our own behavior. Determine how you are going to respond before you confront. If necessary, visualize how a mature person would handle such a situation and play that role. By doing so, you help provide the proper atmosphere for redemption.

> *"An Emotional Bank Account is a metaphor that describes the amount of trust that's been built up in a relationship. It's the feeling of safeness you have with another human being."*
> —Stephen Covey

### Make a deposit

Before we try to resolve conflict, we must ensure that we've made emotional bank deposits. Stephen Covey explains what happens when our account is overdrawn.

> But if I have a habit of showing discourtesy, disrespect, cutting you off, overreacting, ignoring you, becoming arbitrary, betraying your trust, threatening you, or playing little tin god in your life, eventually my Emotional Bank Account is overdrawn.[1]

Redeeming a relationship is less promising when the other person feels like there's little to redeem. Make daily deposits to your most important relationships.

### Establish the right climate

In Chapter 3, we defined how important "climate" is. A climate of hostility and suspicion is antithetical to meaningful resolution. An arrogant or self-righteous attitude distances us from our most important relationships. When our children feel like they have to tread softly around us because we overreact to every failure, they'll probably stop following in our footsteps. The right climate warms homes and friendships.

### Pray before you begin

In Chapter 3 we suggested that we should pray for courage, an open door, maturity, and wisdom. We also recommended praying *with* those involved. When we pray, we not only bring God's power, his wisdom, his presence into the equation, but God uses the process to prepare and clarify our hearts.

### Find the right time

I (Rich) still remember the day I was supposed to be dropping my daughters at their middle school at 8:15 AM so that I could make an 8:30 meeting. Instead, I sat in the driveway loading my emotional canon. Finally the doors flew open, and two happy, energetic girls slid into the back seat. As we pulled out of the driveway, I started blasting away, "Every day this goes on and I'm getting tired of it. When you make me late, I start my meetings late. This makes everyone late for the entire day." I waved a hand in the air for effect; then I looked in the rearview mirror only to see my youngest crying.

"What's *your* problem?" I growled.

My oldest daughter answered instead, "You know what your problem is Dad?

You don't listen to yourself. You travel all over teaching about conflict resolution and the importance of timing … well this is a lousy time to bring this up." She was right. Bringing it up then only made everyone miserable for the rest of the day.

Most of us treat conflict as an emergency, but rarely do we encounter a conflict situation that is. We should avoid resolving conflicts on the way to school or work, late in the evening, on the way to an event, at the table, just before bed, or when one of the participants is already late to something.

Some years ago, I met the Dean of a major university. His president was an avid fan of their football team. My friend confessed that he had learned never to present a new project on a Monday after a defeat. He saved all of his presentations for the Mondays following victories. Here was a man who understood timing.

### Find the right place

At the college where I (Marty) work, there is coffee shop called "Common Grounds." It's the best place to meet "problem" students, because it serves as neutral territory. To observers, we're just having a casual conversation. The setting produces a warmer atmosphere than "the teacher's office" (and the coffee's good, too).

### Communicate effectively

Rehearse and visualize what you plan to say. Choose your words and tone carefully. You may have to write both down. You may even say to the person, "I am so nervous that I would like to read what I want to say." How you say something is as important as what you say. It's best to avoid the following:

- **Dropping clues.** Instead, be specific. Dancing around the problem with comparisons will only cloud the issues and allow the other person to claim ignorance as a way out.

- **Interrupting.** If the other person won't quit talking and you have to interrupt them, let them finish a thought and interrupt at the end of it rather than in the middle.

- **Bringing it up as part of another conversation.** Resolution works best when it is the focus of the meeting. No one likes to be blindsided.

### *Define the problem without personalizing*

Since conflict is personal and painful, it's important to avoid using "you" statements. Define the problem in writing before the meeting. Your note cards should include your contribution to the problem, your feelings about it, how you think the other person sees the problem, what you agree on, and what behaviors would contribute to a solution.

### *Identify alternative solutions*

In a recent meeting with city planners, I (Rich) experienced the advantage of an alternative solution. Our church had been debating how to fund the purchase of additional land for parking. The city planner suggested that if we changed from a suburban church to a city church paradigm, we could save land and money. He said, "What if you do what churches in New York City do and sell a small piece of your existing property to a retailer who would build a multiple story parking garage? He would use the parking during the week and you would use it on evenings and Sundays." It's good to spend time identifying alternative solutions.

### *Decide on a mutually acceptable solution*

When you believe you have a workable resolution, ask, "Does it include practical steps that will actually solve the problem?" Effective resolution eliminates the conflict, strengthens the relationship, and promotes personal growth.

## OUR WORST FEARS

Some relationships are lost because one partner refuses to work on the problem even though the other partner is ready and willing. Consider the following guidelines for engaging the partner who won't engage:

### Guidelines for Encouraging Engagement

1. Ask why the other individual refuses to acknowledge or work on the problem. We can tell you that the most common response is, "I can't face the public humiliation." If this is the case, use the following "Joseph Principle."

   When Joseph, the carpenter, found that his wife was pregnant with Jesus (not knowing, yet, that she had not been unfaithful), he decided to protect her reputation as best he could by divorcing her "privately" (Matthew 1:19).

   Although there was no real conflict (after the angel told Joseph about the miracle of Jesus's conception), still while Joseph was devastated, he reacted with a solution that he believed would lead to healing, not more hurt. You can use the same principle.

2. You may have to get out of harm's way. If you are in a destructive relationship you may have to move out or dissolve the partnership.

3. If you cannot decide on a mutually acceptable solution, be willing to enlist the guidance of a counselor or pastor. Remember the beginning of the book? The reason I (Rich) met with Dave was that my wife called him.

4. Ask yourself what tough love would look like in your situation. If the individual refuses a discreet approach, a confrontation with his family and friends might be in order (only after every other avenue has been walked down).

5. You may have to stay and suffer (see 1 Peter 3:1). Staying and suffering brings us to another consideration—some conflicts redeem us.

## REDEEMING CONFLICTS

Although the first ten chapters spelled out ways we can learn to redeem our relationships, we're not saying that the solutions will erase every conflict—and there's a reason for that.

In his letter to the Christians in the city of Corinth, the Apostle Paul explained,

> We are hard pressed on every side, but not crushed; perplexed, but not in despair; persecuted, but not abandoned; struck down, but not destroyed. We always carry around in our body the death of Jesus, so that the life of Jesus may also be revealed in our body (2 Corinthians 4:8–10).

Whether you are a Christian who believes God is who the Bible says he is or you're simply a curious reader looking for some solutions to relational conflict, it's important to understand that some relational conflict is intended.

### Conflict can draw us to God

If you're not a Christian, it is highly probable that your conflicts are designed to draw you toward God (because He's passionate about you). The Apostle Paul wrote to the Romans, "If you confess with your mouth, 'Jesus is Lord,' and believe in your heart that God raised him from the dead, you will be saved" (Romans 10:9). If you believe the truth in that statement, God has already begun resolving the greatest relational conflict in your life: He's redeeming his relationship with you! If this was your decision, we would like to rejoice with you and help you find a caring, Bible-believing church in your area. (Our contact information appears at the end of the book.)

### Conflict can reveal Christ's character

Certainly, some relational conflict is a direct result of Adam and Eve's choice to sin and not the purposes of God (though he often uses these, too). However, there is a purpose for the other conflicts we experience. Many of them will last until others see "the life of Jesus ... revealed in our body." Understanding how our relational conflicts can show the character of Christ (below) can help us make peace with our pain.

1. **Jesus's humility.** The humility we demonstrate in giving up our wants to solve or reduce relational conflict reveals to the world the sincerity of Jesus's humility in coming to earth and dying on the cross. Our willingness to suffer is difficult to explain in evolutionary terms—it is a reflection of the humility of heaven.

2. **Jesus's forgiveness.** When we forgive, our coworkers, friends, and families are introduced to the wonder of the friend who writes the good we do on stone and the mistakes we make in the sand. These rare responses transcend culture and surprise us as they picture the forgiveness of our Lord.

3. **Jesus's perseverance.** When we work through relationships rather than walk out, we picture for the world the perseverance of Christ. Mel

Gibson's film, *The Passion,* so clearly portrayed Jesus's struggle as he pushed through severe emotional and physical pain to make it to the cross. Our perseverance—our push through emotional and physical pain—points people to his.

4. **Jesus's patience.** When we demonstrate patience the world pays attention. In our Porsche-paced and web-accelerated culture, many people are used to treating conflict like a headache. If it's not gone in the morning, we are! Patience with people stands out—and it reveals the patience of our Creator toward the sinful behaviors that separate us.

5. **Jesus's compassion.** When people see us deeply moved by someone's conflict, they're puzzled. Our world is so much about us, so saturated in sensations that it is hard to be moved by anything. People who are in touch with God's Spirit are reminded of Jesus's compassion for children, the weak, the persecuted, and the ignorant. People who aren't in touch see Jesus's compassion revealed in our demeanor and tears.

Knowing that our conflicts can communicate the character of Christ won't eliminate the pain we feel, but it will help us discover the Apostle Paul's encouragement in knowing that many conflicts provide an opportunity to carry in our body, "the dying of Jesus so that the life of Jesus may be revealed." Rejecting conflict as too painful, too time-consuming, or too intrusive, can mean rejecting the blessing of revealing Jesus.

## The Redeemer of Relationships

If you picked this book up to find a way to help a friend or if reading this book has helped you enough to encourage you to begin helping others, this next section will interest you. As you've probably guessed by now, we have spent years trying to help people redeem their relationships. The best advice we have for fellow counselors like you is the advice we are called on everyday to follow ourselves. It is this: Every redeemer of relationships must listen his or her way to love.

Jesus Christ's own example in this startles us. Why the God-man with all the answers would wait to hear our questions is provocative. But that's just what Jesus did with the woman at the well. Though he knows immediately the answer to her need, he asks a question, listens, and waits for her to ask him for help (see John 4). Why? Perhaps it is because, in knowing all things, he understands that his listening heart will be partly responsible for her healing.

A story that once appeared in a popular magazine tells of a little girl and a single mom who enter a toy store to buy a doll. As the little girl moves down the aisle, she asks her mother what each of the dolls can do. Some of the more expensive dolls walk, others talk, others sing or eat. Finally, the little girl picks up a doll the young mother can afford. But, when she asks what the doll can do, the mother notices there is no description on the box. Then an idea comes to her. She whispers to her daughter, "Honey, that doll listens." Although the little girl knew nothing about the costs of the other dolls, she chose the one that listened. The quaint story of the young child speaks to the child who lives in our heart. Why? Because we still choose people who listen. So do those who are struggling with relational conflict. Listening is a simple, but effective way to help them help themselves.

## Becoming an EAR

Most of us have seen these "conflicted souls" on the talk shows, in the coffee houses, in the cubicles where we work, and through the miniblinds in our neighborhoods. Out of sight and out of touch, these individuals often long for someone who can hear their hearts. Like the girl in the doll aisle, they are waiting for a box that reads, "This one listens." We can help them redeem their relationships by becoming, to borrow the common expression, "all ears." The following acrostic can help.

### E—Enter their worlds

In his book *Caring Enough to Hear and Be Heard*, David Augsburger explains that, for effective listening to take place, we need to learn how to enter another person's world.[2] Entering their worlds will remove some of the communication barriers and help create an avenue for helping them. Sometimes entering their worlds means attending an event with them, reading a book together, or asking questions.

For example, in counseling intellectuals who are struggling with relational conflict, I (Marty) have often found it helpful to use plays from the Modern Theater. Dramas such as *Waiting for Godot* by Samuel Beckett and *Six Characters in Search of an Author* by Luigi Pirandello present the hopelessness of life without God—a hopelessness these people know all too well. Like the pages of the Bible's Ecclesiastes, these plays help us understand those who feel lost in meaningless relationships. Listening to their thoughts about the plays made it easier for me to pray for them and to find bridges we could cross together on the journey toward healing.

## A—Attend the meaning behind the words

"You didn't listen to a thing I said!" How many times do words like these crush a conversation? It's like we're giving an important recital of our thoughts and no one is in attendance. It's important to attend the conversations of people who are struggling with relational conflict. It's important to be there. When we aren't attending the meaning behind their words, our advice can seem like a kind of verbal air hockey. Our words fly back and forth, but seldom touch even the surface of their thoughts and feelings. My wife, Linda, and I have learned that meanings behind our words are different. When I say, "I'm OK," I mean it's a good day. When she says, "I'm OK," it means she wants to talk about something that's troubling her. "OK" can mean different things. It's important to find out what words means when we're trying to help people redeem their relationships.

## R—Respond to their needs

A youth minister friend once told his youth group about the first time he kissed his fiancée. They were sitting beside a quiet stream when he asked, "Honey, can I kiss you?"

She was silent.

Although he considered the possibility that she didn't want to be kissed, he chose to believe she didn't hear him and asked again, "Honey, can I kiss you?"

Still, she didn't respond. Frustrated and wondering if he had already ruined his chances, he nonetheless was so persistent he asked again, only this time louder, "Honey, can I kiss you?"

She was silent. "Are you deaf?" he pleaded.

"Are you paralyzed?" she laughed.

The point is she wanted him to respond, appropriately, to the situation.

After we've *entered* someone's world and paid *attention* to the meaning behind their words, we can *respond* in a way that ministers to them.

This is the same model used by the ultimate Redeemer of Relationships. Jesus Christ *entered* our world, *attended* the meaning behind our words, and *responded* in a breathtaking way to our needs. When we become an EAR we can effectively minister to those who are struggling with relational conflict—we can redeem relationships.

## You Have All You Need — Some Final Words

We're smiling as we finish these last paragraphs (OK, there are a few tears here, too). We've spent five years studying together, writing together, and, of course, praying (and playing) together so that we could fill these pages with the best we've learned. We know these ideas work, but we know, too, that this book never would have been written if God had not, first, taught us these things and, second, orchestrated events so that we could share them with you. That's why it's more than a play on words to say he gets all the glory for *Redeeming Relationships*.

As we've labored to answer questions about ten common relational conflicts, we've presented questions you can ask that can help you move toward reducing their frequency. These we have listed on the following page.

## Key Questions to Help Reduce Relational Conflict

What kind of conflict am I facing?

Is it a shrugger, minor issue, or major issue?

Which factors do I control?

How would others in the conflict describe the problem?

Do I seek to change people?

What about me are they trying to change?

How do I relate to authority?

What kind of climate do I create?

Am I so proud that it's hard to be vulnerable, seek help, or give others the license to tell me the truth?

How caring and compassionate am I?

Do I harbor bitter envy towards others who are more successful?

Am I overly conscious of my rights?

We know that with God's guidance, these questions can help you heal the hurt.

We hope these pages will promote closeness. We hope they will encourage you to leave the shallow end and swim deep into the world of wonder that waits within your relationships. And, finally, we hope that, together, our "oneness" will cause the world to believe that God's intense longing for relationship caused him to send Jesus—the Relationship Redeemer (John 17:21).

**BOLD IDEAS**

When a potentially difficult conflict arises, we pay an emotional price if we give in.

True resolution takes a servant's heart, a loving manner, a listening ear, and an openness to communicate effectively.

The first rule in resolving conflict is to control our own behavior.

A climate of hostility and suspicion is antithetical to meaningful resolution.

Most of us treat conflict as an emergency.

How you say something is as important as what you say.

Some relationships are lost because one partner refuses to work on the problem even though the other partner is ready and willing.

If you're not a Christian, it is highly probable that your conflicts are designed to draw you toward God (because he's passionate about you).

When we demonstrate patience, the world pays attention.

The better equipped you are, the more likely God will use you as an instrument of resolution.

After we've *entered* someone's world and paid *attention* to the meaning behind their words, we can *respond* in a way that ministers to them.

# Notes

## Chapter 1

1. C.S. Lewis, *Reflections on the Psalms* (New York: Harcourt, Brace and World, 1958), 23.

2. John Powell, *Why Am I Afraid to Tell You Who I Am?* (Niles, Illinois: Argus Books, 1967), 88.

## Chapter 2

1. Dr. Henry Cloud and Dr. John Townsend. *Boundaries: When to Say Yes, When to Say No, To Take Control of Your life.* (Grand Rapids: Michigan, Zondervan, 1992), 25.

## Chapter 3

1. Dr. Seuss, *Horton Hears a Who!* (New York: Random House, 1954).

2. Jack and Carole Mayhall, *Opposites ~~Attract~~ Attack, Turning Your Differences into Opportunities.* (Colorado Springs, Colorado: Navpress, 1990), *iii.*

## Chapter 4

1. Dr. Henry Cloud and Dr. John Townsend, *How People Grow, What the Bible Reveals about Personal Growth.* (Grand Rapids: Zondervan, 2001), 9–10.

## Chapter 5

1. Rich Meyers, Mid Valley Counseling Center, personal interview, 28 June, 2006.

2. Paul Coleman, *How to Say It for Couples: Communicating with tenderness, openness and honesty* (New Jersey: Prentice Hall Press, 2002).

3. John Fischer, *Losin' is Winnin': Dark Horse.* Word 1982—LP.

## Chapter 6

1. James MacDonald, *I Really Want to Change ... So Help Me God.* (Chicago: Moody Press, 2000), 14.

2. Stephen R. Covey, *The 7 Habits of Highly Effective People, Powerful Lessons in Personal Change.* (New York: Simon & Schuster, 1989), 70.

3. T. Friberg, B. Friberg, & N. F. Miller, *Analytical Lexicon of the Greek New Testament.* Baker's Greek New Testament Library Vol. 4 (Grand Rapids, Mich.: Baker Books, 2000), 291.

## Chapter 7

1. Charles Elliot Newbold, Jr., "Legalism: The Harlot Church System, Why can't we be friends?" Copyright © Michael Bronson, 2000. http://www.BibleHelp.org

2. ibid.

3. Timothy George, "Evangelicals and Others." *First Things.* February 2006, 16.

4. Philip Yancey. *What's So Amazing About Grace?* (Grand Rapids: Zondervan Publishing House, 1997), 33.

## Chapter 8

1. Dr. Ron Allen. *The Majesty of Man, the Dignity of Being Human.* (Portland: Multnomah Press, 1984), 147.

2. Mark Goulston, M.D. *The 6 Secrets of a Lasting Relationship, How to Fall in Love Again—and Stay There.* (New York: G.P. Putnam & Sons, 2001), 80.

3. Phillip C. McGraw, Ph.D., *Relationship Rescue, A Seven-Step Strategy for Reconnecting with Your Partner.* (New York: Hyperion, 2000) 247.

4. Gary Chapman, Ph.D., *The Five Love Languages, How to Express Heartfelt Commitment to Your Mate.* (Chicago: Northfield Publishing, 1995), 124–125.

5. Mark Goulston, M.D. *The 6 Secrets of a Lasting Relationship, How to Fall in Love Again—and Stay There,* (New York: G.P. Putnam & Sons, 2001), 159.

## Chapter 9

1. "New York Minute," written by Don Henley, Danny Kortchmar, and Jai Winding. (Woody Creek Music Corp/Dobbs Music ASCAP/ 1989).

2. Michael Rappaport, "Are you Drowning in Debt?" *Inland Valley Daily Bulletin,* May 26, 2006.

3. Patrick M. Morley, *The Man in the Mirror, Solving the 24 Problems Men Face.* (Brentwood, Texas: Wolgemuth & Hyatt, Publishers, Inc. 1989), 33.

## Chapter 11

1. Stephen R. Covey, *The 7 Habits of Highly Effective People, Powerful Lessons in Personal Change.* (New York: Simon & Schuster, 1989) 189.

2. David W. Augsburger, *Caring Enough to Hear and Be Heard* (Ventura, CA: Regal, 1982) 38.

# ABOUT THE AUTHORS

**Rich Rollins, D.Min.**, has served as a healthcare professional, college vice-president, and church consultant. He is the executive pastor of Valley Bible Church, a nationally acclaimed community church with a congregation of nearly 2,000 in the San Francisco Bay area. (Approximately 60 percent of the congregation has been saved out of drug and alcohol abuse.) For more than thirty years, Rich's work on relational conflict has made him a sought-after counselor and conference speaker. Rich and his wife, LouAnna, have been married for more than forty years. They have two daughters and a son-in-law, who encourage Rich in his appreciation of golf, jazz, reading, and backpacking through the beautiful mountains of northern California.

**Marty Trammell, Ph.D.**, is Chairman of the English Department at Corban College in Salem, Oregon, and a pastor at nearby Valley Baptist Church. Marty has been nicknamed "Dr. Love" by scores of college couples who have sought counseling from him and his wife, Linda. He has written for the *Chicken Soup®* series, *Research in Christian Higher Education*, and contributed study notes for the *Living Faith™ Bible*, the *Starting Point Study Bible*, and the *Explore New Testament BibleZine*. Marty and Linda have three sons who energize their ministries and help them enjoy music, sports, and cross-country road trips.

Together, Rich and Marty have spent several decades in professional organizations helping repair lives damaged by relational conflict.

Visit our web site at **www.RedeemingRelationships.com** for more information about the authors and how to contact them. You can also subscribe to a monthly newsletter with more useful information for redeeming your relationships.